LITTLE HOME BIG DREAMS

The Tiny Home Lifestyle For Beginners

© 2021 Little Home Big Dreams

All rights reserved. No part of the book may be reproduced in any shape or form without permission from the publisher.

This guide is written from a combination of experience and high-level research. Even though we have done our best to ensure this book is accurate and up to date, there are no guarantees to the accuracy or completeness of the contents herein.

ISBN: 978-1-953714-40-4

Reviews

Reviews and feedback help improve this book and the author. If you enjoy this book, we would greatly appreciate it if you could take a few moments to share your opinion and post a review on Amazon.

Whether you're looking to live in a tiny house on a foundation or a THOW (tiny house on wheels), you're about to have a wild experience. This journal includes daily and monthly thought-provoking prompts to get you excited about your new lifestyle. If you've had a rough day, or just discovered something new about your lifestyle, this journal provides ample room to record all of your thoughts, feelings, and musings about the transitional period.

Go to **https://www.kristine-hudson.com/vanlife** to download it for free.

CONTENTS

INTRODUCTION — 7
AUTHOR'S NOTE: HOW WE FELL INTO TINY HOUSE LIVING — 13
CHAPTER 1: GETTING STARTED — 17
    Section 1: What is a Tiny Home? — 18
    Section 2: The goals of living in a tiny home — 22
    Section 3: Challenges of living in a tiny home — 26
CHAPTER 2: FINDING A TINY HOME — 33
    Section 1: Prefabricated tiny houses — 34
    Section 2: Building your own tiny home — 36
    Section 3: Deciding which version is best for you — 40
CHAPTER 3: LAND, LOCATION, AND LEGAL CONSIDERATIONS OF TINY HOME DWELLING — 49
    Section 1: Building on a permanent foundation — 50
    Section 2: Considerations for a tiny house on wheels — 54
    Section 3: The Legal Bits — 59
CHAPTER 4: SETTLING INTO A TINY HOUSE — 65
    Section 1: Furniture, Tiny-Style — 67
    Section 2: Appliances and Fixtures — 71
    Section 3: Balancing Function and Finishes — 77
CHAPTER 5: *MINI*-MIZING YOUR LIFESTYLE — 83
    Section 1: Reducing possessions and clutter — 85
    Section 2: Keeping your tiny house clean — 94
    Section 3: Tiny home dining solutions — 97
    Section 4: Tips for children and pets — 102
CONCLUSION — 109
RESOURCES — 112

INTRODUCTION

There's nothing wrong with taking up a lot of space. After all, every type of animal has its territory and builds a habitat best suited to its needs.

For some, that's a cozy, warm nest in which to raise our young.
For others, it's an aesthetic network of rooms and halls.
Others still prefer a tiny cocoon to protect and nurture them.

Just as every unique critter has developed its own tastes in homes and habitats, so, too, have humans created a diverse palette of possibilities. Some require palatial mansions or at least one bedroom for each person in the house.

But there's a new trend among modern housing, one that provides a broad sense of flexibility with a strict sense of minimalism. Though those terms sound almost completely polar opposite, there is one housing style that is equal parts wide open spaces and no frills: that of the Tiny Home.

The tiny home lifestyle has a lot of appeal. Much as a cocoon is associated with a certain protective coziness, the tiny home is a shell that provides just enough space to sustain human survival. Every part of the tiny home is strategically planned to be useful, with no corners cut and not a single millimeter unaccounted for.

Many of us are drawn to the idea of having no more space than we need. We're sick and tired of mowing lawns and manicuring the shrubbery. Very few people get a huge kick out of cleaning streaks off room after room of window glass, and keeping the floors clean is a fool's errand.

Add on top of that the giant house payments that come with even a reasonably-sized home, taxes, utilities, insurance ... the list of the financial responsibilities of homeownership seems almost endless.

Apartment and condo dwelling also has its shortcomings. The borrowed space may never quite feel right. In many cases, you lack the ability to make it a true "home," with clauses in your homeowner's association covenants, condo board mandates, or apartment lease preventing remodeling and even painting.

Tiny home living, for many, is the perfect intersection of having a space of your own without having a ridiculously large physical and financial responsibility. We're speaking, of course, in terms of actual size. While the common understanding is that tiny houses come with a tiny price tag, we'll soon discover that isn't always the case. But when it comes to having a potentially portable, bespoke dwelling that fits your every movement, a tiny home is ideal for many people.

Transitioning from a standard-sized two- or three-bedroom house to a tiny house may seem like it wouldn't be a very big jump, but there are many factors that need to be considered before leaving your current home behind.

For many people reading this book, tiny home living is something on the horizon. Depending on the research and exploration you've done so far, that horizon might be years in the future, or you might be ready to write your first check as soon as you put this book down. Regardless of where you are in the decision-making process, you likely have many questions.

There are a lot of steps in the process of finding the perfect tiny house for your lifestyle. But first, you need to make sure that transitioning to a tiny home lifestyle is the right fit for you. In this book, we'll explore the pros and cons of the tiny life. You'll want to be prepared for every challenge and reward that you meet along the way.

Next, you'll need to know how to get started. It turns out that the road to a tiny house is filled with twists and turns and sometimes even trailers. You'll want to be armed with a significant amount of information before you take the plunge on tiny house dwelling.

There are many things you'll want to keep in mind along the journey as well. We'll take you on a room-by-room, or rather pod-by-pod, tour of your prospective tiny house to explore the different things you'll want to factor in, whether you're buying a prefabricated or custom tiny home or building it yourself.

From mortgages to mobility, there are plenty of details you'll need to keep in mind when preparing to leave your house, apartment, or condominium behind for the tiny life. This book is intended to keep those concepts organized so that you have the smoothest move possible. While there will surely be a few bumps and bent nails along the way, you'll be armed with all the information you need to say goodbye to the things you like the least about your current living situation.

Within the pages of this book, you'll find details as to what constitutes a "tiny house," and what you need to keep in mind when it comes to financing, building, and finding the perfect location for your new dwelling. Though the concept of living in tiny homes is growing rapidly in popularity, there are many considerations that haven't quite caught up to the notion, such as insurance coverage, mortgage options, and even finding an appropriate spot to call home. These waters can prove difficult to navigate for the uninitiated, so we'll be sure to walk through each potential challenge in detail.

We'll also focus considerably on the tiny home lifestyle. You may already realize that your giant dining room table isn't going to have a place in your new habitat, but that begs the question: Where are you going to eat instead? What about watching TV or reading a book? You'll need to plan out a space that reflects your lifestyle and provides ample opportunity for you to go about your regular day. This includes tips for minimizing, maximizing, and even making your home feel cozy and personal, regardless of the lack of space.

Lastly, we'll get ready for long-term tiny house living, covering topics such as cleaning, composting, and how to add kids and pets to the fold. Though you may not be able to imagine the possibilities now, we'll share some very helpful tips and tricks that can reduce chaos while amplifying your comfort level in your new home.

This book is written from the perspective of homeowners in the United States, but the concept of making the most out of very little room is universal. With the exception of land, towing, insurance, and financial considerations, the information found in this book can be helpful for anyone looking to maximize their miniature space.

At the end of this book, you'll find a Resources section with links and references to various sources that can help inspire and guide you along the way. You'll also find outlets to the tiny home community. As it so happens, tiny home dwellers have many groups, forums, and sites across the internet where they share new ideas and advice as well as collaborate on new concepts. This community can be invaluable for new members looking for tips, tricks, and a sympathetic ear.

As you read on, you may find yourself wanting to make notes, so feel free to keep a notebook or tablet handy. I very much recommend this method, as you'll find yourself wanting to remember certain ideas and concepts. You'll also be doing a lot of research along the way, so you may want to keep all of your thoughts organized in one centralized area. I refer to "your notebook or journal" several times throughout the text, but I appreciate that most people have "gone digital," so this can mean whatever note-taking, thought-remembering, and dream-capturing method you've established to keep you organized through this process.

You may also be inspired to create a vision board to store some key inspirational notes on a site such as Pinterest. Feel free to do so, as being prepared and aware is one of the best ways to become successful in your transition to tiny home living. The goal of this book is to leave you feeling confident and comfortable in your decision—whether you immediately proceed with your tiny house plans or not.

There is no wrong way to live in a tiny house, just as there's no wrong way to live in a home of any size or configuration. Still, many people who have made the move themselves recommend a certain level of preparation and research before getting too invested in the process. Read on to learn if tiny living is right for you, and how to get ready for the lifestyle changes associated with the switch!

AUTHOR'S NOTE: HOW WE FELL INTO TINY HOUSE LIVING

My own tiny house journey was entirely unplanned and completely unexpected.

If you have read any of my previous books, you'll know that my husband Brad and I have been happily living the van life since 2018. I decided to walk away from corporate America to pursue my dream of being a freelance writer. Brad had been working remotely with the same company for several years. We employed a lot of creativity, made a whole bunch of mistakes, and set out to explore the country in our 1985 Volkswagen Vanagon.

Then came 2020. The year started out pretty normally. We were starting the year by circulating among our friends and families, crashing in their spare rooms or driveways so we could catch up and ride out that holiday spirit as long as possible. Plus, it gave us the chance to drive as little as possible while the weather was still being dicey.

When the COVID-19 pandemic was announced, Brad and I weren't sure quite how to handle it. Living in a van was fine, and relatively low risk, but how were we going to handle the everyday stuff? Grocery stores were running out of food and supplies, campgrounds were shutting down, and city-wide curfews were being enacted across the country. A sense of dread, bordering on panic, set in.

We didn't want to rent an apartment because that would require a lease. Plus, some places weren't even showing or renting to new tenants due to lockdown restrictions. It felt like we were stranded at the end of the Earth with no opportunities to settle down. Think **Mad Max**, only with a lot of stops at gas stations and flavored water.

We considered buying an investment property, then renting it out when we got back on the road again, but that seemed like way too much work. We'd already sold our houses before, and neither of us had the motivation to do any remodeling. We had no furniture, limited supplies, and extremely limited time. Since Brad works in absence management, he was glued to his phone and laptop twelve to fourteen hours every day.

The solution came out of nowhere. One of Brad's work contacts owns a farm in the middle of Illinois. On this farm is a cabin he had recently rehabbed. His idea was to turn it into a vacation rental, but COVID-19 had shut that plan down very quickly. Instead, he asked us if we'd like to rent it until it was practical to get back on the road again.

Initially, I thought the transition from van to tiny house was no big deal. In fact, the extra room seemed downright luxurious. I could sit upright in bed without whacking my head on the ceiling. Brad could be upstairs, and I could be downstairs—we could be separated by an entire layer of space! We finally had running water and electricity and climate control. For the first time in years, I wasn't haunted by sand and gravel that had been tracked into the tiniest corners of the van.

But there are aspects of the lifestyle that are very different from living in a regular-sized house or even a van. Our home is on a fixed foundation, so our travel possibilities are limited. We've even purchased an inexpensive car so we don't have to run errands in the van. Our shower is in a detached building, which we fondly call "the indoor outhouse." The view—which is extraordinarily gorgeous—doesn't change from day-to-day. We have indoor cooking options, but we still like to use the fire pit and grill as often as possible. What I'm saying is that tiny house living will always be exactly what *you* make it. Furthermore, you shouldn't try to force your lifestyle into a tiny house or vice versa. There are so many options and possibilities today that you don't have to scramble and buy the first tiny house you see, even if you're a van-lifer looking for a port during a pandemic.

Thankfully, Brad's buddy gave us a lot of leeway with the cabin. We were able to outfit it in a way that makes sense to us. At the same time, this has given me a lot of time to think about all the things I might do differently if I were to do it again. We've done quite a bit of research into adapting our lifestyle from the van to a THOW (a tiny house on wheels), and it's very appealing to us. That being said, we are going to take our time before we take any next steps and really evaluate where we're going and what we're doing.

This book came out of a place of opportunities and possibilities. I was surrounded by so much research that it seemed inevitable that I would write a book about our journey and share tips and tricks I wish I had considered … or even thought to consider … when we were arranging our transition. As you read on, I encourage you to really take the time to consider what you want and what you need. I repeat that a lot, but truly, think of this as an opportunity to make your dreams come true.

CHAPTER 1: GETTING STARTED

First things first: Before you start giving away your belongings and packing the necessities, let's look at what a tiny house really is. Sure, the pictures online look great, and everyone seems to be smiling and having a good time. But how did they get to this point?

Moving into a tiny home isn't going to solve all of your problems instantly. In fact, living in a new environment is going to provide you with a whole new set of challenges. There are obstacles intrinsic to any type of lifestyle, but in order to find success in a new lifestyle, you have to be aware of these challenges as well as willing and able to meet them head on.

In this chapter, we'll take a look at what a tiny house really is. That doesn't just mean the textbook definition of a "tiny house" but a glimpse into the associated daily trials and tribulations of living in such a space. This book is intended to guide readers through understanding and appreciating the tiny house lifestyle, but I feel it's important to set the scene. There are so many things that are advertised or described as a "tiny lifestyle," so how do you figure out what aspects of that lifestyle you like, don't like, or don't even understand yet?

You're likely familiar with the concept of a "tiny house." After all, the name is pretty self-explanatory. But what defines a tiny house, as opposed to just a really small house? What are the advantages of a tiny house over a small house? Does it differ from mobile home or RV living? Let's take a look at the very basics to answer these questions and to help you get started on your own tiny home journey.

Section 1: What is a Tiny Home?

This is actually a loaded question. There are many factors which go into determining what is and isn't a tiny house as you're soon to discover. You can find a variety of options branded as "tiny houses" online, from 800 square foot cottages, to 600 square foot mobile homes, to portable shacks that seem barely habitable for the long-term resident.

According to the 2018 version of the International Residential Code, Appendix Q:

> "A Tiny House is considered a Dwelling that is 400 square feet in floor area or less, excluding lofts . . . A Dwelling Unit is a single unit that provides complete independent living facilities such as living, sleeping, eating, cooking and sanitation."

The code goes on to define all of the structural requirements for a tiny home, including ceilings:

1. Habitable spaces and Hallways shall not have a ceiling height less than 6 feet 8 inches.
2. Bathrooms, Toilet rooms, and Kitchens shall not have a ceiling height less than 6 feet 4 inches.
3. Lofts are permitted to be less than 6 feet 8 inches. No minimum stated.

Since the lofts are not part of the dwelling floor area, the rules for it are separate:

> Lofts shall have a minimum floor area not less than 35 square feet. Lofts shall not be less than 5 feet in any horizontal dimension.

However, in this case, floor area is not measured in areas where a roof slopes closer than 3 feet from the floor, so a sharply sloping roof can impact this measurement.

While something called the "International Residential Code" may seem like a pretty final authority on building codes, the truth is that codes can vary from location to location. Each city, county, or town can have their own set of rules and regulations for what people can and can't consider a tiny house in their area. In fact, this is possibly the most challenging part of owning a tiny home as you'll see when we discuss topics such as mortgages and insurance.

Additionally, while construction inside the tiny houses is generally less regulated than its footprint, this may be something to start researching now in the pre-planning stages. In the Resources section, you'll find a few links to sites that can get you started finding and understanding the requirements and restrictions in your area.

Remember, too, that these regulations apply to permanent structures on foundations. If you've decided you'd like to live in a THOW (Tiny House on Wheels) you'll not only need to look at structural guidelines but also trailering regulations, the legal requirements for on-road travel, and parking stipulations as well.

Therefore, it's important to start looking and learning right out of the gate before you make any sort of final purchase or decision. Is the home of your dreams considered a tiny home in the place where you'd like to put it? In some cases, you might find that your ideal dwelling is considered a small house.

Does that mean you should put down this book immediately and go back to the drawing board? Absolutely not! Living in a tiny house is all about the lifestyle, and while one municipality might state that you live in a small house, it is still very much your home to enjoy as you please. As you continue to read and research, you'll find that there are plenty of technicalities that will dampen your spirit if you let them. If tiny house living is truly your dream, then rally on! There are plenty of homeowners around the world who have also overcome these challenges to pursue their ideal lifestyle.

Aside from building codes and regulations, the size of your tiny home will be based on your own preferences. According to many tiny home dwellers, there is definitely a learning curve when moving into your new space full-time. They report that one very important consideration is purchasing or constructing a home space that fits your general daily flow. For example, if going up and down a ladder is difficult for you, then a home with a loft bed might not be ideal.

Another fun feature of tiny homes is their unique exteriors. You can find nods to all sorts of architectural styles: from itty-bitty Tudor-style homes with stucco exteriors, to miniature Swiss chalets with high pitched roofs, to log cabins or Antebellum-style abodes that have signature pillars on the porch. There seems to be a notion among those less familiar with the tiny house movement that these are little more than shacks or sheds. Spacewise, it would be difficult to argue against this sentiment. But as far as creating warm, welcoming, functional living spaces, tiny houses are far removed from your regular backyard shed.

As you longingly cruise through online pictures of tiny homes and miniature houses, you may notice that it seems like no two are the same. Many people choose to design and construct their own tiny house from the ground up.

One huge benefit to this is that you will be able to create a space that fits your ideal lifestyle. We'll dive further into the pros and cons of prefabricated homes versus building your own in the next chapter, but for now, keep in mind that you may have more control over the flow of your future home than you might with a three-bedroom house in a suburban neighborhood.

While many of these homes are fully mobile, some are planted on permanent foundations. Once again, codes and regulations are in charge here. There are some locations in which putting a building less than a certain square footage on a lot may not be considered a homestead, regardless of the fact that you have no intention of moving it. There are also locations wherein you can freely construct whatever you feel like building, so don't be discouraged until you've fully explored scenarios in your preferred location.

At the same time, many tiny house dwellers appreciate the mobile option. Many homes have been designed with the idea of being able to load them onto a flatbed trailer and transporting them from location to location based on the seasons or even the owner's whims. The possibility of relocating at any time is often a huge draw to those who appreciate a less rigid and structured lifestyle but still enjoy four solid walls and a roof.

"Versatility" is a word thrown around often in the tiny home community. It refers not only to the structure itself, which can be hauled from place to place with surprisingly little effort, but the interior as well. Without multiple rooms for various purposes—such as a bathroom, bedroom, and kitchen— each space must be versatile. As you leaf through the examples on Instagram or Pinterest, you'll notice an eating area can double as a desk, or a seating arrangement unfolds to become a bed. There's a certain amount of flexibility that comes with tiny living.

That flexibility needs to be reflected in each individual owner as well. This is not to say that you need to be able to do a backbend to get into the bathroom but that you are not the type of person who requires large spaces for languishing. You need to be okay with being able to touch every wall with your arms outstretched, depending on your interior design. Therefore, before you get started, it's important to understand why tiny living is a thing, and whether you're on board with the overall goals and results that can be found in such a unique way of living.

Another thing to keep in mind as you proceed through this exercise is whether you really want a tiny home or just a small space. Micro apartments and condos do exist and might be an option to consider before you go all-in on a tiny house. There are pros and cons to these dwellings of course. You won't have the freedoms available from owning your space, and taking your house on the road with you is definitely out of the question. You'll have to share walls with neighbors, and in some cases, smaller apartments have bigger issues.

The exercises in the following sections will help you appreciate the "whys" of your desire to live in a tiny home and, hopefully, extract some of the deeper thoughts and feelings related to the topic. While we may be tempted to just do it, the topic of homeownership and planning for the rest of your life deserves a little deliberation. Read on to discover the pros and cons of tiny home living, and consider how these changes will impact your lifestyle.

Section 2: The goals of living in a tiny home

There are many positive rewards for living in a tiny home, most of which can be classified under the umbrella term "saving." Those who live in tiny houses will be saving space, saving money, and saving the environment in the long run. That being said, the advantages of living in a very small dwelling aren't always outright and abundant.

As you are defining your proposed tiny home lifestyle, always bring yourself back to the reason you want to do this in the first place. Why do you want to ditch the neighborhood and go tiny?

There are likely several reasons which extend beyond the pesky shrubbery and steam cleaning acres of carpets. While those are certainly big-time motivators for trying your hand at minimalism, there are multiple solutions for those issues that aren't quite so life-altering or permanent.

Therefore, as you loudly object that you really *do* want less space, ask yourself again, "Why?" What about your life would change dramatically if you were to leave your current abode and live in what many people proclaim to be "a glorified shack?"

The romantic and aesthetic appeal are often towards the top of the list when it comes to reasons people want to try tiny house living. The consolidated interiors look fantastic. If you're not wasting a single inch, then there aren't huge, ugly light fixtures, or awkward unused wall space. In a tiny home, everything truly has a purpose. The deliberate details that owners put into these homes can be a huge draw for those who have lived their entire lives in unimaginative houses or apartments.

There's a certain dollhouse element to the aesthetic as well. Tiny houses are twee and resourceful, with a "waste not, want not" outlook that combines function with looking cute. And owners decorating the outsides as very small castles, log cabins, or Swiss chalets proves that they are meant to look as cute as they come across.

The consolidated lifestyle echoes the simplicity that we all crave in life. Life is incredibly hectic for many of us. Eliminating as much stress as possible has become a survival technique; in a sense, we're all trying to save ourselves from any stressor that can be easily eliminated. Our superfluous stuff, the feathers that pad our nests, can be soothing and stressful, sometimes all at once.

Would you feel more comfortable in your home if you didn't have to walk past that awkward bare spot on the wall? Would you feel less anxious if you didn't have to keep your vast collection of knickknacks in tip-top shape?

We all have things that we collect, and many of us go into collection mode when we're very stressed out. There are loads of psychological concepts and motivations behind this behavior, such as wanting something positive to inspire hope in our lives or to have a physical reminder of the time and effort we have put into a certain task evidenced by that big splurge we often make after a particularly large work bonus or overtime check. But do we really need that stuff, or is the burden of caring for that stuff making our stress worse?

In a tiny home, it is virtually impossible to collect things, regardless of how subconsciously your brain may make purchases. You'll find yourself growing more and more creative as you divest your collections of this and that.

Think about putting all of your favorite geegaws in a single desk drawer. All of them. Can you do that? More importantly, do you want to do that? Nearly everyone is capable of narrowing down their collections, but when you attempt this exercise, how do you feel? Accomplished? Or maybe you feel a profound sense of loss. Either reaction is perfectly valid, but if you find yourself grieving your belongings, perhaps a different type of minimalism is in your future.

Echoing the teachings of Henry David Thoreau, withdrawing to nature with only the most basic of necessities can restore balance to your peace of mind ... right? It turns out, there might be something to that "hippie-dippy nature stuff." If you choose to build a tiny home on a permanent foundation, you may find yourself getting creative with zoning laws and property lines. If you build a THOW, you'll be able to pick up and move on a whim. Being in control of your location at all times can be a very freeing experience, allowing you to retreat to your own version of Walden Pond and come back to civilization as you wish.

Of course, as mentioned earlier, there might be some legal red tape and hazy legality on that location front too. Still, you'll definitely use fewer utilities, even if you were to set up your tiny house in the backyard of your current home. It would be impossible for a tiny home to require as much energy and water as a full-sized house, so you're guaranteed smaller bills.

You can also go completely off-grid if you feel like it. Thanks to advances in generators, composting toilets, water tanks, and solar power, a tiny house can be rigged to be completely self-sustaining in a sense. You'll still need to empty the toilet and change out the greywater tanks, but your tiny home can be as efficient as any camper van or motorhome. If you choose a permanent location that's appropriately zoned for it, you can even grow a garden, collect rainwater, raise chickens ... the sky's the limit!

But each time you find yourself getting excited about these prospects, dial back to asking yourself "Why?" You can start a garden nearly anywhere, thanks to container solutions and indoor grow stations. You can fit most homes with solar panels, and if you really felt like it, you could use little to no electricity at any time. So what is it about doing so in a tiny house that gets you more excited about these concepts?

For those who happily live in tiny homes, the winning combination is a little bit of all of these categories. Choosing your own location, off the grid, with minimal distractions, and living in a fully self-supported manner sounds like a challenge to lots of folks, but many see this challenge as a dream come true.

Section 3: Challenges of living in a tiny home

So what are the downsides to living in a tiny home? Sure, it sounds like the local and legal stuff can be a bit of a hassle, but in a perfect world, what could possibly be bad about living in a tiny house?

It turns out that just because a space is small doesn't mean it requires less upkeep. True, it will not take you very long to sweep a house the size of your current bedroom. That being said, you may find yourself sweeping every single day or even multiple times a day.

Just because your home is tiny doesn't mean the dirt somehow shrinks too. If you wear muddy boots into your tiny home, your dirty footprints will need to be cleaned up right away, lest the dirt should track further and further into your home. Parents of very small children are familiar with this phenomenon, but for the uninitiated, every tiny little mess will magically spread before your very eyes. You'll notice dust more easily too. Not only will you be able to see it with your eyes, but if you have allergies, you'll definitely feel the effects.

One thing that many people aren't prepared for when they make the switch to tiny houses is the frequency of cleaning. In a standard-sized home, you can do things like leave an empty glass on the coffee table overnight or save doing the dinner dishes until morning. Granted, the people who raised you might have a thing or two to say about such habits, but let's face it, none of us are perfect housekeepers.

In a tiny house, however, you're almost forced to be a near-perfect housekeeper. One rule of thumb of leaving things out is that it's going to stink or get in the way. That cup of cold coffee sitting in your sink will not only make the entire house smell like coffee due to the small confines of space, but it's most likely going to take up your entire sink space.

Furthermore, certain cleaning activities are going to be a lot different in a tiny house. Next time you make the bed in your current bedroom, ask yourself how your process would change if the bed took up the entire room. Where would you store your clean sheets? How would you wash your sheets? What kind of weird yoga positions will you need to practice to both strip your bed of the dirty sheets and put clean ones on? There are actually videos (linked in the Resources section at the end of this book) of tiny house residents demonstrating tasks such as these, which folks who live in standard-sized houses take for granted.

Let's go back to the coffee cup example. So your dirty coffee cup is in the sink, and you've decided you want a nice cup of tea. You reach for another cup, perhaps a clean cup in your cabinets … but wait! This is a tiny house. You don't have loads of kitchen cupboards filled with cookware and cutlery. Living with very little space means that just a few items will fill that space. That's not to say that you have to use itty-bitty teacups and teeny-tiny plates, but if you choose to have a twenty-piece dinnerware set, you will need to sacrifice other just-as-necessary items to make the space for it.

Minimalism is key when it comes to tiny house living. You'll need to become very keen on things that can be used for multiple purposes and finding ingenious storage spots for things that aren't being currently used. Later in this book, we'll look at methods for minimizing your belongings without going completely bare, as well as explore some ideas for making the most of your space. For now, look around your house and get a feel for how much stuff you wouldn't mind getting rid of. Is this exercise challenging, or are you pretty okay with the idea of having a giant garage sale or donation party?

Another thing to consider is company. Do you like to have your friends over for dinner parties? Are you the type who likes to lounge out on the sofa with your buddies for movie night? Depending on the layout of your new home, that may or may not be difficult, but there are other things to consider about hanging out with your friends in your tiny home: Bathroom use, for example. Additionally, it might be tough to find places to hang all the coats and stash all of their shoes, depending on the weather. And if your kitchen is limited in cups and cutlery, will you ask them to bring their own if they come over for dinner?

When you're first considering tiny home living, these challenges might not seem like a big deal. It's all part of the experience, right? Absolutely. But before you get super-invested in planning for your small home switcheroo, really think about your lifestyle. What are some things you're willing to sacrifice? More importantly, what are some things you're definitely **not** interested in changing?

There are solutions to all of these challenges of course. With a little foresight and planning, you'll be able to troubleshoot and accommodate. Just like any major lifestyle change, things will feel awkward and maybe a little uncomfortable at first, but you'll come to find your stride over time and continue to learn and grow into your tiny home.

However, if any of these challenges seem like it may be too uncomfortable, this is a good time to explore that situation more. You might feel that your concerns are ridiculous, but it's far better to address a ridiculous concern now than to invest all of your time and money into a tiny house you'll ultimately not enjoy.

One common exercise to help you understand whether or not you'll like tiny house living is to mimic the scenario. There are a few different ways to do this:

1. Live in your bedroom for a week. For the purpose of this exercise, it's ok to use your bathroom as you normally would but try not to leave for any other reason. Cook all of your meals in your room, do all of your daily tasks in your room, and limit yourself to the items you have in your room. This means you'll have to plan ahead and pack everything you think you'll need for the week in your bedroom. This isn't going to be exactly identical to the tiny house experience, but you'll get a feel for your wants and needs in a small space, which is a great place to start on your tiny house journey.
2. Rent a small RV or camper van for a week. Again, not exactly the same, but there are several things you'll learn from this experience. First, you'll gain an appreciation for living in a space in which every square inch is designed to be fully functional or even multi-purpose. You'll get insight into how much space is available for storage and

movement as well as ideas on how to maximize your minimal belongings. You can also get accustomed to using a composting toilet and greywater system, which are very common among the tiny house community.
3. Try renting a rustic cabin or tiny home for the weekend. Some campgrounds or holiday resorts actually offer tiny home rentals on their grounds. This can be a risk-averse way to find out not only if you're comfortable with the lifestyle but can also give you some ideas about changes you'd make to the layout or flow in your own tiny house.

If you choose to complete one of these exercises, you may wish to keep a journal to make notes about the experience. Notice what changes about your daily routine when your living space is diminished. Are you finding yourself wishing you had more space in a particular area? What are some things you didn't fully plan for? What are some surprises that came up along the way? Make notes about what you would change if this was your entire living area and reflect on the experience often.

At this stage of the game, you still have plenty of decisions to make. Even if you are 100 percent green-lighting the move to a tiny house, your best move at this point is to start the research and weigh your options. While most of us hate the anxiety and anticipation of a long, drawn-out process, this is one area in which having patience and doing the legwork before you make a huge investment can pay off big time.

If you're like many people preparing for a major lifestyle shift, you're probably near-obsessively cruising sales sites, social media, and watching all the television shows you can regarding tiny homes in order to prepare. This is definitely a good idea, as the more exposure you get to the concept, the more ideas and knowledge you'll have as you creep closer and closer towards your own dream home. But remember: a lot of what you see on television has been scripted and edited for entertainment value. Social media posts are filtered to look good for the viewer. What you're seeing is a fully scrubbed, filtered, and viewer-friendly peek into a much more complex reality.

We're not saying to avoid these outlets of expression; on the contrary, it's a great opportunity to see a variety of different styles, options, and choices made by others who have traveled a similar path. But if you're going to embrace a tiny house lifestyle, that means taking it all in. In addition to researching fun things, like storage solutions, look at less-exciting necessities, like toilets and greywater systems. In addition to looking at pictures on Instagram, follow some frank and honest blogs too. A few options have been included in the Resources section to help you get started on this search.

In the next chapter, we'll look at what it takes to find exactly the right tiny home, including the pros and cons of various construction options. While it may be incredibly tempting to pull the trigger on the first functioning tiny house you see, remember that this is more of a process than simply moving your belongings from one place to another.

Many people like to keep a journal or notebook during a huge life change like this to keep track of their thoughts and ideas. This is a fantastic idea, especially if you're trying to juggle your regular lifestyle on top of making changes. If you choose to do so, here are some topics to really consider at this stage of your tiny home journey:

- Why do I want to live in a tiny home?
- What do I need to take with me?
- Where do I want to put my tiny home?
- What are some things I love about the tiny house lifestyle?
- What will be more difficult about my lifestyle in a tiny house?

As you read through the next chapter, you can also use this journal to make notes about tiny houses you like, features that you love, and surprises that you find along the way. You want to make as many notes as you can at this point, because as your new lifestyle takes shape, you'll want to revisit your thoughts and opinions. Don't be surprised if they change frequently too. The more you learn about tiny house living, the more you'll appreciate taking the time to get organized now.

CHAPTER 2: FINDING A TINY HOME

Finding your very own tiny home and locating a place to put it are equally important, which is why we've devoted a full chapter to each topic. It's a little bit of a "chicken and the egg" scenario. As stated earlier, there are plenty of laws and regulations which dictate the minimum square footage of a permanent home which can prevent you from simply buying a lot in any old neighborhood and throwing up your tiny home.

At the same time, knowing what type of tiny home you want is going to help you narrow down where you can put it. For example, if you decide you want an A-frame on a foundation, you'll be able to specifically research locations where that's permissible and go from there in choosing your exact plot of land, finding a lender, builder, insurance, and so on.

Some folks may find that purchasing a tiny house before you have a plan for locating it is very much putting the cart before the horse, and we couldn't agree more. The purpose of this chapter isn't to encourage you to rush out and make a purchase as soon as you're done with the last section but instead to help make you aware of the options that are out there. There are prefabricated tiny homes, build-your-own kits that can be customized, shipping containers or school bus conversions, and there's even the option to just go for it and design and construct your own home from the nails to the shingles.

Therefore, the purpose of this chapter is to provide a practical introduction to all of these options so that you can personally weigh the pros and cons of each before you take the plunge. You'll be able to decide what you want, what you can live with, and what you definitely want to avoid before you put down that first payment. From here, we'll guide you through choosing a location and looking at the legal aspects, but first, let's take a look at some of the most common types of tiny houses to get you started on your research.

Section 1: Prefabricated tiny houses

"Prefabricated" or "prefab" is used to describe houses that have already been constructed. These houses already exist and can be purchased "as is."

When it comes to tiny houses, there are actually a few different versions of this. For example, there are actual tiny houses that have been built over the years and exist as permanent structures in towns and cities around the world. We tend to think of this type of structure as a recent phenomenon, but you'll find very small cottages and 600-square foot and under homes dating back to the early days when your area was settled. After all, the first structures of any civilization weren't elaborate three-bedroom split-levels with basements and central air!

If you're interested in a historic tiny house, you'll need to do a little research. That means searching through real estate listings until you find something that meets your needs and dreams. They aren't impossible to find, but they may be located in out-of-the-way areas. If that's part of the draw of tiny homes for you, then you're definitely on the right track.

To start looking for an already-existing, permanent-on-a-foundation, someone-has-already-lived-there tiny house like this, head to the online real estate sites. Many of them provide search criteria such as square footage and location, so you can get a feel for what options might be available. You may not find exactly what you're looking for, but you will be able to get a feel for the market in a particular location.

You'll also have the option to shop new and pre-owned tiny houses on wheels. A good place to shop for these is online forums for tiny house enthusiasts. We've included a few links to some websites that can point you in the right direction in the Resources section at the end of this book.

There are many pros and cons to choosing a prefabricated or pre-owned tiny home. Most importantly, bear in mind that your house will already be completely constructed. If you're shopping for your first tiny house, and you're not particularly handy or well-versed in structural codes and the construction process, this might be a great starting place for you, since everything has been laid out in careful consideration for codes and creating an ideal living space for many homeowners.

However, this also means you will have very little opportunity to modify or customize your new house. A smaller footprint means that everything is purposefully built in its place for a reason, so attempting to update one feature, such as counter space in the kitchen, may require an entire remodel of the entire building.

On the other hand, some people purchase a prefab structure without interior walls for the purpose of doing a complete remodel of the inside space. Many of the code regulations that apply to tiny houses specifically mention the exterior of the dwelling, so having an exterior that adheres to local regulations can help you get your foot in the door of a tiny home (pun intended).

So while a prefab tiny house can be updated, it may be a lengthy, strenuous process. It will require expert understanding of construction and engineering, as well as tools, lumber, and other supplies. You'll need to have a place to live while you're doing the renovation, since the small space more or less precludes being able to live under the roof while you're making updates.

Then there's the overall cost. Already built houses will always cost more than a load of lumber and a building permit. Since you're buying an existing structure, you'll want to be aware of the price per square foot as well as any relevant taxes. You may want to shop around a location to make sure that the price is fair and that you're not being taken for a ride due to the oddity of the commodity. Still, if you're purchasing an already standing home, it may be easier for you to secure a mortgage and insurance, especially if it's on a foundation and has been for quite some time.

Section 2: Building your own tiny home

The second option is to build your own tiny home. Much like purchasing a prefab house, there are different ways to accomplish this goal. The choice you make depends on how hands-on and do-it-yourself you are willing to be as well as how much time you have to dedicate to the process.

Remember, once you get started, you're going to have to follow this project to the end. That means you'll need to have a dedicated timeline for construction and completion. This timeline can vary greatly, depending on your budget and level of expertise. You'll want to ensure you have a place to live while you complete construction and plenty of time budgeted for mishaps and other calamity.

Time spent and money spent often go hand in hand when it comes to budgeting for a tiny house build. If you're building the entire dwelling on your own, you'll need to pay for every bent nail and stripped screw that goes into the process, and that can add up to lots of dollars and lost time if you're not extremely confident and competent in your construction skills.

However, there are a few options which can assist on this front. Many hardware or lumber outlets have created tiny house kits. Some of these simply include detailed plans and instructions for your build, while others actually include pre-cut lumber and fittings.

Naturally, these kits range in price, depending on the complexity of the build and the contents. They are very convenient, and in many cases, already rated to code—meaning they already meet the guidelines for housing. Much like with the prefab houses, you might lose a bit of customization, but you'll know you're getting a safe, livable house with all of the storage and function details already thought out for you.

You can also create your own plans and build your tiny home from scratch. If you choose this path, research is extremely important. Many things work very well on paper yet somehow don't translate well to reality. We've all seen construction fails with doors that don't open correctly, stairs that lead to walls, and toilets that are close enough to the front door that anyone can peek in. Before you create your own miniature Winchester Mystery House, make sure you really pay attention to all of your measurements.

You'll also need to be super diligent about construction codes in your location. Building a tiny house only to not be able to live in it would be truly tragic though an important and expensive life lesson. Rather than face the heartache of having a useless structure on your hands, self-builders will need to be fully informed. In fact, it may be helpful to hire a contractor or engineer experienced in tiny house building to help you navigate the process.

Another interesting option you have when constructing your own tiny home is a choice in materials. Our tiny home is constructed out of reclaimed materials. The lower floor was a one-room log cabin constructed in 1865. The builder tried very hard to salvage as much of the original structure as possible, but whatever couldn't be reused in the construction of the current tiny house went towards another project, and he substituted decommissioned telephone poles in their place. Even the cabinets are constructed from a barn that previously stood on his property.

When you choose to build your own tiny house, you definitely have greater control over the plans, the utilities, the appliances ... essentially every aspect will be hand-picked for your needs. In the case of our current home, this allowed the builder to reuse perfectly good parts and pieces for a very green, very cost-efficient tiny home construction process.

He confirmed that this required a lot of effort though. Not only did he have to find all the right pieces of lumber, but he had to find someone who was willing to do the cutting, since he lacked the space and equipment to turn telephone poles into planks.

Since you aren't just making a major run to a hardware store, you may also find your project stalling while you refurbish a particular piece. Alternatively, you can search for the perfect salvage item to finish your current area of building.

So if you're not the most patient person, or you have a timeline by which you need to have your tiny house in livable condition, using strictly salvage items may not be the best option for you. Remember, there is no right and wrong, as long as you're meeting the local building codes and requirements. If the roof stays on in rough weather, and the doors open and close correctly, then you've got the hardest parts of the process under control. But if it really is important to you to use salvage materials and green, sustainable construction processes, then bear in mind that you might have to extend your timeline and prepare for delays.

Lastly, you'll need a place to build it. Unlike a bookshelf or coffee table, this isn't a project that will fit in your garage or rec room. Sure, certain parts can be constructed independently from the full structure, but at some point, you will have a fully-constructed tiny home shell that's ready for drywall, plumbing, and electricity. Where are you going to put all of these parts, and more importantly, where are you going to put them all together?

Much like renovating a van or RV, building a THOW will require room for the "wheels and up." That means you'll either construct your home on top of the trailer and build from the wheels up, or you'll construct your home first, then lift it and secure it to the trailer. Either way, you'll need to have a space that has clearance enough to fit an entire house. The other dimensions are also important, but height is an added component that truly needs to be considered. Building a tiny home that won't be able to leave the garage can be a very complicated problem!

As far as the location itself, you'll want a spot that has access to power or a reliable generator so you can use your tools and spotlights as needed. You'll also need plenty of space for construction as well as the ability to store and lock up things like small fixtures, tools, and metal, lest they wander off in the middle of the night. Some localities have very strict rules about putting up another structure on the same lot as a house, regardless of how temporary the setting may be, so before you throw up a tiny house in your backyard, find out if that's legal in your area.

Once you have a location set for construction, make sure you check out the noise ordinances. Your after-work build may be shut down after sunset, depending on where you live.

All in all, there are a lot of factors that go into determining whether a self build or kit-born tiny house is right for you. Making the ultimate, perfect-for-you, absolutely custom tiny house of your dreams with your own two hands is a beautiful goal and one many people hope to accomplish. However, it may not be the right time, place, or solution given your budget, your needs, and your deadlines.

Always weigh all of the facts along with the pros and cons of constructing your own tiny home. There are many emotional components to the process, but always be aware of the legal, practical, and financial aspects of your decision before you become too invested in your project.

Section 3: Deciding which version is best for you

As you can see, the path to living in a tiny house is lined with choices and decisions. At this point, your brain may be swarming with details and facts, things you like and don't like, and option after option that you find on the internet.

The system of organization you've developed is going to come in particularly handy for keeping all of these swirling thoughts in line. It's time to pull out the journal or notebook to get these thoughts jotted down before they spiral out of control or start swarming around noisily.

You've already examined why you want to live in a tiny house. You've taken the time to consider what features about this lifestyle appeal to you and some of the areas where you know you might have a harder time adjusting. You may feel that this list is no longer important, once you've green-lit your decision to move into a tiny home, but it's actually going to be very relevant to every choice you make going forward.

You see, everything that you have identified as a challenge when it comes to living in a very small dwelling can be manifested by the space you choose. As an example, let's say you indicated that you are intimidated or unsure of having a loft-style bedroom. You don't like the idea of crawling down a ladder if you have to go to the bathroom in the middle of the night, and you're absolutely certain you're going to crack your head on a pitched ceiling if you wake up suddenly. If you choose a space that has an elevated sleeping area and a steep roof, that challenge will continue to magnify itself every time you go to bed.

Alternately, let's say your soul-searching led you to discover that you aren't comfortable dealing with a composting toilet. Honestly, they're not that fun, and this is a completely reasonable discovery! In this case, maybe a THOW isn't the right idea for you, and you'd be much happier in a tiny historic home or apartment. The beautiful thing about all of these myriad choices and decisions is that, eventually, the pieces will align to create the perfect home for you.

Unless you are on a specific timeline, such as a job relocation, it's a good idea to take your time searching for a tiny house. In a regular-sized house, you can make accommodations for things you don't like without a giant disruption. In a prefabricated tiny house or tiny house kit, though, it's going to be much more difficult to repurpose or remodel an area, since all of the pieces and areas are specifically created to work as one.

At this stage, take the time to think about what you require from your tiny home. You've likely seen a lot of floor plans and layouts, so use those images to help you jot down a list of all of the things that you know you need and that you absolutely don't want. For example, some tiny houses have galley-style kitchens, while others have a flow-through lower level. Despite what some Instagram photos would tell you, not all tiny houses have a loft. Do you want a loft, or does that seem problematic for your particular lifestyle? Do you want an actual bathroom, or are you okay with an RV-style shower-with-a-toilet-in-it water closet?

If you discover that some of these things really aren't a priority to you, make note of that as well. Maybe you don't care if you have a porch or not. Perhaps windows aren't really something that concerns you because you plan to spend most of your time outside anyway. Conversely, you may want as many windows as possible because you don't want to use a generator for electric light. There truly are a ton of options to consider at this point.

This is your dream, so you're allowed to really think about what qualities you want your dream home to have. You may have to compromise on some of these things, but listing them out now and discovering what your priorities are will make the tiny house shopping process that much easier.

Once you've got your wants and needs identified, start shopping. Some people recommend starting shopping for exactly what you want. Personally, I find this to be a great way to become quickly discouraged and disappointed. When you're starting out, starry-eyed, dreaming big, things will look fantastic on paper only to not live up to expectations in person.

Therefore, I recommend looking at everything. At the very least, looking at something that you are pretty sure you don't want will help solidify your feelings that this is not the right choice for you. You may feel like looking at a tiny apartment is a dumb idea, because you definitely know you're leaving the city, but think of the space as a source of hands-on inspiration to help guide your list of what you definitely want in your very own space.

And, yes, that goes for those of you who are adamant about building your own tiny home as well. As mentioned earlier, there are kits and plans available, but you're still going to have your influence on this structure. You'll want to pay attention not only to the layout to ensure it works for your lifestyle, but by looking at existing models, you'll get a feel for a variety of floor plans and layouts and experience a lot of different innovative built-in and customization options.

Since innovation and customization are two of the tiny home tenets, these are definitely things to pay attention to. Things like cutting boards or desktops that slide in and out of countertops like a drawer help combat the lack of flat space in the kitchen, which can be a huge help if you like to take time to carefully prepare meals. Each time you look at a new tiny house, make notes in your journal about these features. Even if you have a visceral negative reaction to a space, it's still taught you something very important about your preferences and will guide your ultimate tiny house decision.

I recommend jotting down detailed notes before and after checking out each space, whether you do so in person or virtually. It doesn't have to be anything anyone else would even understand but enough information that when you revisit these notes later, you'll know exactly what you meant.

For example:

House #1

Square footage: 302

Built: 1865

Construction: FIXED FOUNDATION. Log cabin, rehabbed 1994 to add windows, tin roof, electric circuitry.

Price: $159,900

Notes: Open floor plan lower floor. Composting toilet/utility room under stairs. Sink in the kitchen area only. No interior shower (separate shed). Wood burning stove. Solar powered rain collection system. Solar panel electricity. Small furnace. Former fireplace updated into cold pantry with cupboard. Built-in bed upstairs.

House #2

Square footage: 225 + 89 in loft

Built: (custom, upon request)

Construction: THOW, Tumbleweed "ROANOKE 26' Alta"

Price: Starts at $78,000

Notes: Fully mobile. Queen sleeping area in loft, and queen sleeping area in flex room. Closet in a great room and loft. Under-stair washer/dryer. Counter space and shelves in the bathroom. Overhead shelves in kitchen with optional oven/optional microwave, cooktop and hood included. Stairs to loft. Flex room could serve as an office or great room space.

House #3

Square footage: 396

Built: (custom, upon request)

Construction: THOW, Tiny Portable Cedar Cabins, "Townsend Cottage"

Price: Starts at $68,000

Notes: Two full bedrooms with a bath off of the central kitchen/dining/living area. Full kitchen oven/hood/sink/fridge. Few standard built-ins. Room for custom storage options. Ceiling fans. Lots of natural light. Very flexible kitchen/dining/living area. Could repurpose the second bedroom as storage/office.

House #4

Square footage: 203 (150 sq. ft. main, 53 sq.ft. loft)

Built: PLANS ONLY

Construction: Kit, built on steel trailer, 84 Lumber, "Countryside"

Price: $500. (Includes list of materials, framing, sheathing, and cladding diagrams, floor plans, interior & exterior elevations, overall sections, and structural sheets. Emailed upon purchase.)

Notes: Built-ins include under-bench storage, desk/table surface, kitchen cabinets, exterior storage bins, full bathroom, storage under built-in ladder to loft, windows in loft for light/ventilation, cooktop/sink/mini-fridge in kitchen. Loft is large enough for a queen-sized mattress only.

This may feel like a lot of examples, but these are four actual real-life tiny houses. As you can see, the array of differences really is stunning. On top of that, the three that aren't pre-built can be completely customized with the finishes you prefer.

Looking at these four examples, which tiny house are you drawn to? What do you like about them? What do you find less appealing about each one?

There are no right or wrong answers to these questions, only features and options that are right and wrong for your lifestyle. The goal of a dream home is that you aren't faced with any nightmares when you actually live in it, so take this time to plan carefully and research everything.

If a kit house looks good to you, for example, drill down to learn more. What are the user reviews like for the kit? Is it easy to build? Has anyone noted any complications? Does it include helpful hints for construction? Has anyone had difficulty getting insurance based on these plans? Are there recommendations for appliances/electric/water/plumbing included, or are you expected to source that information separately?

What about a construction company? What types of experiences have others had with the company? Will they build anywhere or allow you to purchase the building specifications? Can you pick up your THOW once it's built or have it delivered? How will you check on progress? What type of trailer is required? Where are they based? For example, a company based in New Mexico may have different priorities for building than a company based in Minnesota based on the typical weather for each location.

The questions for each type of tiny home are seemingly endless. Because of all the variations and differences between them, it's hard to come up with a full troubleshooting checklist for every tiny home you may encounter. Two prefab houses or two THOWs may be so very different all while still having many of the options you've included in your list of wants and needs. This is why I highly recommend looking at as many as possible before you make your final purchase.

Above all, when it comes to choosing your very own tiny home, trust yourself. You know what you like. You know what you need. You will know if climbing up and down a ladder to go to the bathroom late at night is a good idea for you. There will be options that you look at and immediately say, "NOPE." If at all possible, take your time shopping around and drill down to get as much information as possible. If you don't have the option to visit the houses in person, look at as many pictures as you can, preferably those in which the home is staged to look like it's occupied. How many chairs fit in the seating area? How big is the refrigerator? Are there pictures of the bathrooms?

If you look at photos and cannot imagine yourself living in that space, then it is likely not the right space for you. Remember to include a link to photos in your notes and explain to yourself why you don't like it. This can make it so much easier to narrow down your choices in the long run, leading you to the ultimate logical decision.

In the next chapter, we'll look at considerations like land permits, mobility requirements, and details like insurance and utilities. These are all definitely parts of the tiny house experience that you'll need to consider before you make your final purchase.

There are so many moving parts and pieces to the tiny house equation that you may start feeling hopeless and defeated at times. This is absolutely normal. As noted at the beginning of this book, it's not a simple process, and you will have to do some legwork to make sure you're completely legal. However, every dream requires some dedication before it comes true. The information is out there, and there are plenty of individuals in the tiny home community who are more than happy to help you along the process. Resources are bountiful, and if you find yourself getting frustrated by dead ends, remember that there are so many different roads to try next. Let your notes and your dreams be your guide, and don't be afraid to reach out to others in the community to help you find your way.

CHAPTER 3: LAND, LOCATION, AND LEGAL CONSIDERATIONS OF TINY HOME DWELLING

Of course, having the ultimate tiny home of your dreams won't be entirely possible unless you have a place to put it. You'll also need to make sure you can pay for your house, that you can insure it as is required by your state or location, and that you can legally obtain the resources you need to make it run, like electricity, water, and heat.

This is also where most of the difficulties lie in the tiny house dilemma. You see, some areas have restrictions on how big or small a vehicle on wheels can be. Does it or can it come off of the trailer? Some locations consider them a mobile or trailer home, while others consider them RVs. In some places, it's not ok to park an RV at a trailer park and vice versa. Even if you own the land, there might be regulations about what's considered a permanent structure.

Then you get into the legal bits, like getting a mortgage or loan, and trying to insure the finished product. Is it a house or a temporary structure? Is it considered a recreational vehicle or a permanent dwelling? Do you insure the house and the trailer together or separately? Do you need a CDL (Commercial Driver's License) to tow it around? And, if so, does that mean you need to get commercial vehicle insurance? Is it even legal to haul on the freeways? Depending on your location and where you plan to go with your tiny house, the list can go on and on.

Therefore, it would be impossible to address every single if/then scenario when it comes to the legal implications of building, living in, moving, purchasing, and insuring a tiny house. Consider this a high-level overview of some of the things you might not have thought about when it comes to tiny house living. The ins and outs can be very complicated, and there may be overlapping and conflicting information, depending on your location.

While we can't give you all of the ins and outs for the exact tiny structure you want to live in, we can point you in the right direction for what to consider and where to go for more information. The links in the Resources section will guide you to great starting points, regardless of your location or destination. Additionally, the chapters in this section will help you learn how to ask the right questions in order to get all of the answers you need.

Section 1: Building on a permanent foundation

You might think, *well, if I own the land, then I can do whatever I want, right*? In some places that's true. Either the building codes and zoning laws for that area are very lenient, or the community has decided not to enforce them.

But if you've ever accidentally tangled with a Homeowner's Association (HOA) in the past, you'll know that some communities take these regulations very seriously, down to the tiniest pink flamingo.

Earlier, we discussed building codes. Generally speaking, most locations will want to know that any permanent structures being built meet the International Residential Code (IRC) and/or the International Building Code (IBC) requirements. The next thing you'll want to check are the Zoning Regulations. These can be mandated at the federal, state, and local level. You're likely familiar with some of the broader implications of zoning, which designates certain areas as residential, commercial, agricultural, and so on. But these guidelines can also require certain types and sizes of buildings on lots.

For example, some areas consider tiny houses to be an accessory dwelling unit (ADU). This might be the case if you're putting up a cottage or granny pod in addition to your current home but can prevent you from **exclusively** building a tiny house on your property. You may have to research ways to get around this, such as constructing a tiny house that meets the recommended square footage for a single-family detached dwelling in that county or township. Some folks have gotten around this requirement by constructing another structure, like a barn, workshop, or garage that meets the zoning laws. So while you may need to be creative, there are work-arounds. You just might need to be a little innovative. Again, this is why taking the time to do research is so very important.

Then there's the matter of utilities. Some localities require all single-family permanent structures to be attached to the municipal water sources and sewage system. Since part of the draw of having a tiny home is the ability to live off the grid, regulations such as these may cramp your style. On the other hand, that does mean you won't have to deal with the composting toilet, which might be a bonus, depending on the lists you made during the last chapter's soul-searching exercise. Of course, just because the connection exists doesn't mean you have to use it.

Remember the historic tiny homes we discussed in the previous chapter? Sometimes these get away with their existence due to homestead laws or historic building registries. Given the complications that would be involved in bringing these structures up to requirements that were established long after the dwelling was constructed, these homes tend to get a pass on zoning and code specifications. That's not a blanket statement, though, so always be sure to double-check, even if your prospective tiny home has actually been on its foundation since the beginning of time.

The following checklist should help you organize some of the requirements, restrictions, and legal nuances that you'll encounter when attempting to construct a tiny house on a foundation on your own land:

1. Locate the zoning requirements for your state, county, and township. You may need to consult with a building professional or do some digging on the local auditor's website. There are some leads to get you started in the Resources section of this book, but you're going to want to be very detailed here.
2. Double check the address of your land with the zoning map.
3. What are the local zoning requirements for a single-family detached home? Start at the state level, then the county level, then look at the requirements for the specific zoning code for your lot.
    a. What is the minimum permitted square footage?
    b. Can the home be constructed inside city limits?
    c. What building codes must be met for the structure?
    d. Is it considered the main building or an ADU?
    e. Will you need to hook up to utilities?
    f. What building codes are enforced in this area? (e.g., size of rooms, hallways, windows, ladders/stairs)
    g. How are these codes enforced?
4. Now, take a look at the tiny home prospects that meet your needs and wants. Which will work? Which will require modification? How difficult will these updates be?

This is another good time to pull out the notebook or journal to keep details organized. This checklist may look pretty straightforward, but there's a lot of fiddly details involved.

For example, in my home state of Ohio, tiny houses aren't specifically addressed on the state level, but at the local level, there are many variations on the requirements. In some areas, like metropolitan Cleveland, primary residences under 950 square feet are not permitted. You can have an ADU, but it can't be your permanent residence. In Oklahoma, however, tiny houses haven't even been addressed by zoning laws, so it's kind of a free-for-all. In some areas, including parts of Florida, entire tiny house communities have been established, where only tiny houses can be constructed, but then a few counties away from these tiny havens, you can't have a small detached residential structure at all.

This may seem like a lot of legwork, and to be honest, this is the most complicated part of transitioning to tiny home living. You may feel more comfortable consulting with a housing or building expert in your area to ensure you're looking at all of the right requirements correctly. The last thing you want is to have your dreams dashed because your loft ladder has the wrong tread width.

On the other hand, you might read this section and feel relieved that you're not interested in a permanent dwelling. Keep in mind, THOW regulations are just as complicated. Read on to find out how to keep your mobile tiny home legal.

Section 2: Considerations for a tiny house on wheels

In many places, a tiny house on wheels (THOW) is considered a recreational vehicle. However, this is not always true.

Therefore, if the THOW life is calling your name, the very first thing you should consider is the legality of the size and shape of the structure you are hoping to call home. In the previous chapter, we took a look at the idea of tiny house kits and professionally designed tiny houses. One of the major advantages we discussed is that these plans have already been vetted by professionals to be up to code.

When you have a THOW, you not only have to worry about where to park your recreational vehicle, but the matter of transportation becomes a concern. Typically, a tiny house that measures under 8 feet 6 inches wide, 13 feet 6 inches tall, and 40 feet long will meet the Department of Transportation trailer regulations without requiring a special permit. But that doesn't mean all of the roadways you wish to explore will be accommodating of those measurements. Low bridges, thick tree growth, and narrow back roads can make traveling with your tiny home extraordinarily treacherous.

Some THOWs are permanently constructed on a trailer base, such as the 84 Lumber kit mentioned in the previous chapter. Others are adapted to be moved with a trailer but can slide off and on the trailer rig, much like a traditional mobile home or a pop-up camper rig. Each version has its share of complications and benefits.

If it lives on a trailer full time, it's very likely your THOW will be considered an RV. That means you may encounter difficulties in parking it. The dimensions may not adhere to local RV park guidelines, especially if you have a loft or second level. At the same time, local ordinances may prevent owners from parking an RV on the plot of land you own for more than 30 days. There are designated RV parks around the country, many of which have space for permanent residents. However, these parks may have regulations surrounding tiny homes, despite the structure being legally defined as an RV in that area.

Mobile homes are typically defined as greater than 400 square feet in size and in most locations must have the wheels up, removed, or immobilized when parked. If your THOW is permanently attached to a trailer, this will be impossible. That may prevent you from being able to set up your new home in a mobile home park too.

Now, before you throw up your hands and give up, remember that you are not the only person who has ever encountered all of these seemingly endless, conflicting guidelines. There are plenty of places where tiny homes are welcomed or even ignored. Take a look at this chart with plenty of options to consider:

Option	Pros	Cons
RV Park/Tiny Home Community	• Will have the resources you need • Welcoming • Understands tiny house challenges • Sense of community	• May have parking limits • May be hard to locate • Not off the grid • Can be crowded • May have more rules and regulations to follow
Federal Land	• No one will disturb you • Completely off the grid • Fully legal • Can explore at will	• Can be hard to locate • May be impossible to get a THOW parked there • Still have regulations on length of stay
Rural Plot of Land	• You own the land • Off-grid in many aspects • Great way to be self-sustaining from a food aspect	• Still subject to property taxes • Zoning applies, but may be loosely enforced • Some utilities may be required • Limits ability to explore
Flying Under the Radar (aka: Doing What You Want)	• Park and travel however you want • Completely off-grid • Only have as much social immersion as you want • No land costs or parking fees	• Risky • Need to be aware of consequences • May require packing up and leaving immediately • May have legal/tax consequences

This list is not all-inclusive, of course, and depending on where you stay (or roam), the pros and cons may be more extensive. However, this should give you some perspective on the options that are available to you and some of the things to keep in mind when pursuing those options.

Another thing you'll need to keep in mind as a THOW-dweller is your tow vehicle. As someone who has done a lot of work for the automotive industry, I could go on all day about GVWR (Gross Vehicle Weight Rating - a detailed measure of the weight of a vehicle and everything in it) payload, towing capacity, horsepower and torque, and what to look for in a vehicle to tow your tiny home. At the end of the day, however, you're going to want to purchase a truck that you feel comfortable driving, that you can afford, and that makes sense for your lifestyle.

In fact, you may not want to buy a truck at all. When it comes time to move your THOW, you do have the option of renting a truck or contracting with a hauling company to move your home for you. These are going to be pretty pricey, of course, but if you have no reason to own a truck besides occasionally moving your tiny house, they would be far less expensive than letting a Heavy Duty truck sit around unused.

Depending on the size of your house, a half-ton truck may be sufficient. This includes models like the Ford F-150, the Silverado 1500, or the Toyota Tundra. However, if you are new to trucks, the number one thing you need to know is that not every model is going to have the same towing capacity. Oftentimes, the cab/bed configuration, axle ratios, and engine choices will impact the overall towing maximum. You'll also find different numbers for traditional hitches and gooseneck hitches. When searching for a truck, look specifically for the maximum towing figures and what configurations, options, or accessories are required to reach that number. Most full-sized trucks will offer a comprehensive towing package that will give you the best features and towing numbers possible.

If your tiny home size or weight requires a Heavy Duty truck, double check that you won't need a Commercial Driver's License (CDL) to operate it. In most cases, the truck itself can be operated with a regular driver's license but pulling an entire house behind it may change the game.

Always pay attention to the hitches. A traditional trailer isn't going to connect to a gooseneck and vice versa. There are also a wide variety of hitch classes and possibilities. You'll need to make sure the brake wiring and electric is properly connected too. Some trucks will be able to handle only a small portion of hitch classes, while others can take on a variety of loads. Ask questions about every truck on your list of options to ensure you've got the right equipment.

Cab size is another consideration if you have children or pets joining you. Many times, regular cab models will have the highest towing capacities, but these vehicles generally only seat two to three people. A larger cab with a backseat may make more sense for your lifestyle but can also compromise your towing capacity.

The good news is that this information is not difficult to find. A quick internet search of the year, make, and model will give you the towing specs. If you're buying a new or pre-owned truck from a dealership, you'll be able to discuss your towing requirements with the staff who will have all the figures you need to keep you and your tiny house safely on the road.

The last thing to briefly mention when it comes to hauling a THOW is the actual traveling itself. As mentioned earlier, narrow roads and low bridges may become problematic depending on the height of your THOW. But there are other practical implications of pulling a house—gas stations, for example.

A lot of fuel stops in the US have overhead roofs that may be an obstacle for a tiny house with a loft. Tight turns can also be cumbersome or even dangerous. Jackknifing is a real concern, and the aerodynamics of your tiny house may make driving in high winds or rain terrifying. Therefore, you may want to throw into your list of THOW considerations having to mpa out and preplan your routes to ensure safety along the way.

You'll definitely want to take the opportunity to learn how to drive with your trailer. Basically, this will require a lot of practice in a low-risk area. Additionally, you may look for trailer-friendly features in your tow rig. Modern trucks have all sorts of equipment on board to assist in trailering, from auxiliary switches that operate trailer lights and features, to cameras that help you see in and around the trailer as you drive. These features should not be considered cheating; instead, they are very important ways to keep you, your family, your home, and everyone on the road as safe as possible.

Section 3: The Legal Bits

I'm the type of person who really likes to take care of everything on my own. I love digging into the research and finding all the fussy details that make things work. That being said, there is absolutely nothing wrong with consulting with a professional when it comes to what I call "the legal bits" of tiny house ownership: the financing and the insurance.

Getting a loan in the United States isn't too terribly difficult. Even with bad credit or no credit, you can generally find a creditor to provide you with a sum of money, though the interest rate on said loan may take your breath away.

The good news is that tiny houses traditionally cost less than full-sized houses. In fact, you can build a tiny house for as little as $10,000 if you put your mind to it. However, that $10,000 space might not be perfect for you. Additionally, most of us don't have five to six digits worth of savings that we can wantonly spend, which means some type of lending or mortgage will be required to get fully invested in your tiny home.

Unfortunately, that drags us right back to the "is it a house or an RV?" question. RV loans exist but may not permit using the structure as a permanent dwelling until the loan is fully paid off.

You may be thinking, *well, they'll have to catch me and prove that I'm living there*. And that's true. That is a roll of the dice that some tiny home dwellers are willing to take, especially in the fly-under-the-radar style of living. It's risky, for sure, and the penalties differ depending on the lendor and the location.

You can also search for non-traditional lending. Besides crowdfunding opportunities, there are actually quite a few online investment methods that are based on non-traditional, private loans. Again, there are various levels of risk associated with these programs, and only you will be able to vet how comfortable you are with the risks and rewards.

Your best bet might be financing your tiny house as a primary or secondary residence. The requirements for these types of loans again vary between financial institutions, and you'll need to do some shopping around to find a loan that best fits your needs. Therefore, keep the following in mind when searching for the right loan for you:

- What is the interest rate?
- What does the monthly payment look like?
- What factors can impact the monthly payment?
- What is the loan period? (How long do you have to pay it off?)
- Does the lending party consider your tiny house an RV or a permanent structure?
- What's in the fine print?
- What are the stipulations of the loan and the consequences for disobeying these stipulations?

Remember, if you're buying a THOW, you might be looking at a loan for a truck to haul your prospective home in addition to purchasing the home itself. Is there a way to combine the financing through one institution? Frequently, auto dealerships provide their own financing for vehicles, but that doesn't mean you're required to use their resources. See what can be consolidated for the best rate and lowest monthly payment.

Frequently, the loan and the insurance go hand in hand. Naturally, if you're still making payments on the structure, your lender will want to know that they can recoup their money in the event of a disaster. The challenge comes in making sure your loan and your insurance match up.

You may need to explore a variety of options when it comes to insurance. Since your tiny house might be considered a recreational vehicle, you'll likely need to insure it as such. But RV insurance isn't intended to be insurance for a permanent dwelling either. The rates and coverage are based on infrequent use of a temporary residence. The greater the usage, the greater the risk. Therefore, you might need to look into a rider to provide additional coverage for the full extent of the structure and the contents.

If you're on a permanent foundation, it's more likely that you'll be able to finance and insure your tiny house as a primary residence, but the coverage still may not match the reality of the home. Property insurance is designed to cover liability and structural damage for a full-sized house and often is calculated based on square footage and construction materials. The goal is to be able to reproduce your house nail for nail and stud for stud, based on current market costs.

Property insurance also takes into mind the location of the house. Considerations such as weather risks (like tornados or hurricanes) and physical concerns (such as large trees that can blow over or uneven terrain) can impact your ability to get an insurance policy as well.

While all of this is pretty standard in the insurance industry, it can be a real pain if you're trying to fly under the radar with your tiny home. As a veteran of the insurance industry, I would recommend against trying to commit insurance fraud, however inadvertently, and be honest when you're working with the insurance company. You can actually save a lot of money, time, and frustration if you're up front with your agent or officer.

If you are going mobile, make sure you have coverage for the trailer and truck as well. Some states require trailer insurance in addition to RV insurance, but it's relatively inexpensive and provides more liability coverage during transit.

I also strongly recommend shopping around when it comes to insurance as well. Whether you're doing an online quote or sitting down in person with a representative, provide them with the structural details of your tiny house, including square footage and construction details. Be upfront about how you plan to use your tiny home, including how often you plan to travel, where you want to go, and whether you're going to be on or off-grid.

As I mentioned earlier, you might want to get a professional involved, especially if all of this is unfamiliar territory. There are tiny house experts who offer their services consulting on each and all of these topics. You'll want to make sure they're the real deal before you pay them for their services, and make sure you're comfortable with what they're doing. Additionally, there are plenty of guides and communities that can help you navigate the waters. Remember that every person is going to have a slightly different experience so take their advice with a grain of salt. Still, knowing you're not alone as you make these difficult decisions and conduct seemingly endless research can be immensely helpful throughout the process.

You may be feeling completely overwhelmed or frustrated at this point in the process and rightly so. But before you throw in the towel on your tiny house dreams, think about this objectively. Is it any more frustrating or strenuous than purchasing any other type of home? Are the complications in the process due to your unwillingness to compromise or from an external factor? If external, what type of accommodations can you make to work within the guidelines presented?

In the first chapter, we looked at all of the draws of tiny house living and your own hard and fast requirements for making it work. When you find yourself growing frustrated, consider visiting those lists or concepts again. Are your preferences evolving and changing as you go deeper and deeper down the rabbit hole? It very well might be that now is not the time for your tiny house adventure. You might need more time before you can make it happen the way you want, or more money, or a more accommodating location. Just like any other major transition in your life, a lot of things can change between the first inkling of an idea and the actual realization of your dream.

Therefore, I recommend you stay calm, stay organized, and when in doubt, research it out. Frustration comes from a place of emotional disruption, and while it's perfectly natural to have a lot of feelings about completely changing your living situation, the best way to combat these feelings is with facts and logic. You are absolutely allowed to cry and yell and fuss when things don't work out on the first try, just as you are encouraged to celebrate the victories along the way. However, when you feel you've hit a wall, take several deep breaths and head back to the drawing board with all of your facts in hand.

CHAPTER 4: SETTLING INTO A TINY HOUSE

Now, here's where we push the fast-forward button a bit. In the first chapter, we took a look at the pros and cons of tiny house living and completed a few exercises to help you determine if you're really ready to take the plunge into the tiny house lifestyle. Next, we looked at the different types of tiny houses and some of the advantages and challenges associated with each. Chapter 3 is intended to get your thoughts and questions sorted out when it comes to additional considerations about living in a tiny home and get you started down the relevant research path before you finalize your plans.

So then what happens? Slowly, but surely—or perhaps in a blazingly fast and furious sweep—you make all of your decisions. In my case, I had little input into our tiny house. It was there. We loved the set up. It was within our budget. Everything lined up much faster than I ever intended. But this is the exception, not the rule. In retrospect, I wish I had had enough time to prepare, because the next several months involved fiddling around a mostly unfurnished house with my husband, trying to figure out what we were doing, and where we were going with this endeavor. Time is a luxury, and if you can afford it, take as much as you can!

Once you have your plan settled, it's time to execute. That might mean printing out plans, buying supplies, and driving the first nail into your new home. It may mean driving your newly purchased truck out to hitch up your professionally constructed tiny home, ready to drag it to wherever you plan to spend your first night. It may even mean chasing out the bugs and rodents so you can move into your 1800s cabin. It all depends on how intrepid you are and what decisions make the most sense for you in the end.

Regardless of where your choices lead you, it is now time to pad your nest, so to speak, and establish the new patterns of your new lifestyle.

We've taken a look at how all of the space needs to be superfunctional, but what about the things you put in your home? The thing about the comforts of home is that they're supposed to be comfortable. But, in a tiny home, you don't have room for that overstuffed sectional or the king-sized therapeutic mattress. So how do you adapt?

Furthermore, you're going to have to do functional house stuff in order to sustain yourself—that means appliances and bath fixtures. Your tiny home may come with appliances, and if you've purchased a construction kit, you might have recommendations for what appliances you should put in there. But, as always, you do have a choice as to what to keep in your home. Plus, what do you do if you need to replace something?

Lastly, you've got to establish a flow in your home. This is going to take time and be largely experiential. You may find that the way you thought you would use your space is very much different from the way it actually works. However, the process can be a little more nerve-wracking than it typically is in larger houses.

You may be thinking, *I'm pretty sure I can figure out how to use my house without reading a book*, and I am completely confident that you can. However, making a transition from a larger house (where you can just close the bedroom door and stretch out on the bed for some private time) to a tiny house (where you have to climb up into the loft and do some light yoga to get into bed) can be a bit of a shock the first few times.

If you've grown accustomed to sacking out in front of the television after dinner every night, where are you going to do that now? Where are you going to put the television?

If you work from home, where are you putting your work area? What types of surfaces and seating do you need to get your job done, and how do you consolidate that with all of the other activities you do throughout the day?

I thought that living the van life would prepare me for tiny house dwelling. After all, I knew how to do a lot of stuff in a little space. However, it wasn't until we actually moved into our tiny house that Brad and I discovered that our van-life success had depended a great deal on having the outdoors to work with. Establishing outside areas can be helpful for your tiny house lifestyle as well.

The goal of this chapter is to help you consider all of your daily ins and outs so that you can adequately prepare your tiny home for your move-in day. There will always be a learning curve for figuring out how things work. No one can help you establish a flow; it just comes with time and experience. However, you can start thinking about some key elements of your lifestyle now and how to best reflect that lifestyle in the interior of your new tiny home.

Let's get started turning your new tiny house into your dream home!

Section 1: Furniture, Tiny-Style

We've already established that your full-sized eight-person dining table and sectional recliner sofa will most likely not fit in your tiny house, but the considerations for furnishing your new home don't stop there.

Take a look around at your current home. What kind of furniture do you have? You might have a dining table and chairs, a sofa, some side chairs, a coffee table, and perhaps some lamps. Try to adjust your gaze. Look at them from a perspective of not how useful or comfortable they are, but in regard to how much space they take up. Your everyday dining chairs may suddenly look enormous. Lampshades take up an incredible amount of space. Additionally, the square footage on your rugs may astound you.

Now, you can take measurements of all of your existing furniture to see how much square footage it actually takes up. For many people, that is an extremely helpful exercise. You can compare that to the actual measurements of your tiny house to figure out what will fit and what will not.

An option that's also effective but requires less math is to start with your floorplans and then consider your needs. Take a look at the actual space and then consider how furniture will actually fit. Or you can flip that and look at the space from the perspective of your needs, then determine what tools are needed to make that space do exactly what you need it to do.

Regardless of how you approach your furnishings, you're going to need to consider size, shape, and function, not just of the furniture, but of your overall space. There's a bit of a jigsaw-puzzle feeling when attempting to make the whole equation work. This is why furnishing a tiny house is much more challenging to many people, compared to a regular-sized dwelling.

Start with the part of the house that's most important to you. If having a cozy area where you can rest and relax is most important to you, start in the bedroom. If creating and enjoying home cooked meals is a priority, start with the kitchen and dining area. If you know that you're going to lose productivity unless you've strategically created the perfect workspace, then start there.

I truly do recommend approaching this like a jigsaw puzzle, trying out different pieces in different areas to see if they have that *just right* fit. Let's say you know you want a flat surface for your laptop, and you need a chair that's going to provide back support while you work. So you start with the workstation. Consider that the flat surface you use for work can also be used as your dining space. What area has the best lighting so you don't have to squint at your computer screen? Is there room for the chair you need there? Can that chair also function as a lounge chair in the evenings? Or is there another area more suitable for lounging?

As you can see in this example, the puzzle pieces flow from one area to another. Everything is connected in a tiny house, because you can't just tuck your office chair in a corner when you're not using it.

For another example, let's look at the 84 Lumber "Countryside" model, which was House #4 in Chapter 2, Section 3. Please note that I'm not specifically endorsing this model. I've never seen it in person, and I have no ties with 84 Lumber or any of its affiliates. This particular tiny house has won several accolades for its design, so I've done a lot of analysis regarding what works in this particular plan.

One thing that stands out in the living space of this model is that it's equal parts living space and kitchen. The kitchen may be in small, RV-like proportions, but all of the traditional components are there, from appliances, to sink, to countertops.

Take a look at the living space. There's a high countertop along the windows that can be used as a desk or eating space. Directly across from that is a bench-style daybed with under-seat storage. This could serve as a lounging/sofa-type area, or you could pull up a TV tray and eat there or work there; this is truly a flexible living space that can serve multiple purposes.

In this type of floor plan, the only furnishings you would really need are chairs for the dining and work-surface space as well as a bed for upstairs. The design of the floor space in this particular model really limits your ability to add things like chairs and coffee tables, though, on the plus side, the built-ins cover many needs.

Compare this, then, with some of the other plans you can find online. Some might have fewer built-ins in the living area, which means you have greater flexibility for creating your own dining/working/lounging space. Some tiny houses may have one large room, while others have a separate flex room/area where you can set up an office, second bedroom, movie room, or whatever your lifestyle requires.

Does tiny house living mean you'll have to throw out all of your furniture and start over? Well, yes and no. There are some things that will clearly not fit. There are some things that you can reasonably make work. Moreover, there are other furnishings and fixtures that will make the transition with you perfectly.

In the next chapter, we'll look at the process of minimizing and keeping your lifestyle minimized. But, for now, prepare to part ways with some of your larger furnishings, either through donation or yard sale. While this can be bittersweet, it's an important step in writing the next chapter of your life.

Section 2: Appliances and Fixtures

If you are purchasing a prefabricated tiny home of any sort, or you've purchased a kit that includes appliance recommendations, this part will already be decided for you. Your kitchen and bathroom will already come equipped with plumbing, electricity, and the fixtures necessary to cook and keep yourself clean.

That being said, you may need to replace those at some point in the future. Whether you change your mind regarding the types of appliances and fixtures that came with the tiny house, or something breaks, or you end up wanting to make your free-wheeling lifestyle more permanent, there may come a time that you need to look for new appliances and fixtures.

It's also worth noting that if you're building your own tiny house, you'll be looking for these items for the first time.

It can be kind of intimidating, shopping for tiny appliances. This is one instance in life where size really matters. Not only do you have to make sure that the appliance or fixture fits in the spot where you want to put it, but you need to make sure that it has the ability to function properly with your electric and plumbing set up.

In our tiny house, we have a regular-sized microwave, a small refrigerator that fits perfectly under the kitchen counter, and a one-cup coffee machine. We have three overhead lights downstairs and one lamp upstairs. We also have two outlets for charging laptops, phones, and devices, and a furnace that provides intermittent heat when the temperature drops below a certain level. We specifically chose these items conscientiously with the capacity of our roof-mounted ceiling panels in mind.

When it comes to electricity and plumbing, your tiny house may be very similar to a camper, motorhome, or other RV. Unless you're built on a permanent foundation, or the zoning requirements indicate you must be hooked up to the local sewer and power grid, you have a lot of freedom in this regard.

Living off-grid is a very large part of the tiny house draw, especially for those who elect to put their house on wheels. Since utilities are often a huge part of our monthly expenses, whether we rent or own our homes, transitioning into a tiny house is going to create a fantastic opportunity for savings. The limited opportunities for using power and water are going to drastically reduce your need for these commodities.

Even if you do end up staying at least partially on the grid, you're going to notice a big difference in your utility expenses. After all, you can now theoretically light your entire home with a single light bulb.

So now it's time to continue making decisions to fill your house with the necessities. Are you going to have electricity in your tiny house, and if so, where is it going to come from?

Most THOW setups have either a generator system or solar panels. There are pros and cons for each power source. Generators can be loud and require fuel, which can disrupt the whole green living concept you might be going for. They also require maintenance and attention to ensure they're running safely and correctly over time. Still, they can be very helpful for providing long-term reliable power, especially if you're going to keep a variety of devices charged.

Solar panels require no fuel, are generally pretty silent, and aside from checking on them from time to time to ensure they're still properly fastened to your roof or walls, require no maintenance. On the other hand, they are pretty expensive to install, and when they stop working, the panels have to be completely replaced rather than repaired. You may not have power on demand, either, if you choose to park your THOW in an area that's shady, rainy, or if you need to work during the dark hours.

There is, of course, the little-bit-of-both option, in which you install solar panels, but bring along a generator for those just-in-case times. This can be a little easier in a tiny house setup than in other forms of RVs, depending on how frequently you plan to move your THOW.

Ultimately, the type of appliances you choose will need to be suitable for your power source. It may be difficult to run a full-sized refrigerator on the number of solar panels you can fit on a tiny house. Take stock of your actual electrical needs. Are there places where you can choose a non-electric power source?

Your phone and laptop will likely require a power source to keep them charged. How about your refrigerator? Cook top? Water heater? Electric kettle? Will you need or use fans or heaters to keep your tiny house cool or warm, depending on the weather outside? Are you going to have a television, radio, or projection screen? What about an alarm clock? There are so many ways that we use electricity without thinking about it, which makes it very important to have these appliances considered before you move into your house and need to re-think some crucial requirements.

If you can live without electronic devices, then consider yourself quite lucky, and move on to your lighting. Tiny houses can be designed to have plenty of windows for natural light, but there are a few tricky spots. First, if you are in an area that is cold or windy, your windows may impact how warm you can keep the inside of your dwelling. Then you'll have to think about a heating source, which might also require electricity. And, of course, natural light is not always available. Though there are some areas that experience 24 hours of sunlight from time to time, there will be darkness and dimness nearly everywhere you roam.

Battery-operated lights, such as flashlights and tap lights, can be very helpful, especially in small areas that don't need a lot of light, such as the bathroom or sleeping loft. Battery-operated appliances and tools are becoming increasingly prevalent, so it's very likely that many of the resources you need are available without a plug. You'll need to stock up on batteries, of course, but if your usage is minimal, this is a pretty cost-effective off-the-grid solution to creating light in the dark.

Lanterns, wood burning stoves, and propane camp stoves are excellent non-electric solutions for your household, as well, but remember that open flames and small spaces aren't always the best mix. Make sure you have plenty of ventilation, as well as the appropriate fire extinguishing equipment when using these types of tools. An external cooking area, such as a grill or a firepit, can be another solution to cooking without electricity.

If you do choose to set up your kitchen with appliances that require electricity, be conscientious about how much power you can use at once and how much each appliance requires. Some tiny houses have real-and-true kitchens with gas stoves and ovens, while others have electric burners built into the counters. Always check your load capacity and make sure that it's alright to run the electric kettle, the burners, and charge your phone at the same time. Otherwise, you'll plunge into darkness with cold water, cold dinner, and limited phone capability.

Refrigeration without electricity is possible though somewhat tricky. Brad and I used an old-fashioned ice chest in the van, which did the trick and kept things cool. On the downside, we've melted a lot of ice, and we've definitely lost a lot of delicious food due to water leaking into containers or ice melting faster than we could replace it. Unless you'll be moving around a lot, and thus have constant access to ice, I wouldn't necessarily recommend the ice chest method. Thankfully, you can find refrigerators in nearly every size and power supply, from those that can stay cool with a charge from the car battery to under-counter RV and dorm-sized units that can pack a surprising quantity of supplies for the size.

Then there are the fixtures that require water, such as sinks, showers, and toilets. Another thing to consider is laundry. Some tiny houses have room for a miniature washer and dryer, but those will require both electricity and a water source. You may prefer using laundromats or washing your clothes by hand and air drying them whenever possible. One quick note about that: there are some areas where using an outdoor clothesline is prohibited. While you're looking at zoning details, double check to see if there are any requirements for clotheslines before you accidentally put your unmentionables out for all to see!

Unless you are connected to a foundation and public water/sewer system, you will be using water tanks. Much like in any other type of RV, you'll have your dirty water, your greywater, and your freshwater tanks. That means you'll need a source for your fresh water, whether that's through rain collection sources or from the public spout in your tiny house community.

The good news is that these types of water systems have very few costs associated with them. Once you've purchased the tanks and have a reliable source of fresh water, you're pretty much good to go. You'll need regular maintenance to ensure all of the pipes and pumps are functioning properly, and you definitely need to stay on top of managing your black water and greywater tanks, but this type of system is definitely an "it is what it is" type of scenario.

Speaking of "it is what it is," there are some sacrifices that must be made when it comes to water usage. Using a composting toilet may take some getting used to. Putting a time limit on your showers may require some adjustment as well.

For me, washing dishes by hand has never become easier, though I may be perpetually in mourning for my full-sized dishwasher. Still, you will very quickly become more aware of how many dishes you are using and ensuring they're washed as soon as you're done using them. Between the clutter, the smell, and the bugs and rodents that appreciate a good crusty plate, the consequences of not cleaning up as soon as you're done with a meal will become immediately obvious.

The final thing you'll need to consider is how you're going to pack all of these utilities away. In a standard-sized house, you generally have a basement or designated utility room where your hot water tanks, fuses/breakers, and furnace are stored. Depending on what options you choose for your power and water sources, you'll need a place to store your generator, water tanks, and more.

In our home, that's all stashed under the stairs with the composting toilet. It is a very tight squeeze. We have debated moving the toilet into the shower shed, but the idea of dashing out of the house and across the lawn in the middle of the night is equally unappealing. You would think that living in a van for as long as we did would have hardened us, but there are some aspects of our suburban upbringing that we haven't quite reconciled with our lifestyle and passions yet.

Once you have the furnishings and fixtures determined, it's time to make it all functional. That means taking a look at your space and figuring out how it will work for you. That also means creating an aesthetic that makes you feel like you're at home without cluttering up the place.

Section 3: Balancing Function and Finishes

I am a firm believer that your home should reflect what you need and want it to be. As a writer, I need my space to be quiet yet inspirational. I need separate areas for focusing on my work as well as for relaxing. I see a blank wall as a threat, not a peaceful, meditative area. I like unique, colorful artwork that takes my mind and my imagination on wild journeys, but I also appreciate endless views into nature.

In a tiny house, there's not a lot of extra space for knickknacks, artwork, or colorful expressions of personality, but it's not impossible. There are plenty of ways to incorporate your personality and self-expression with regular functionality.

In our home, for instance, the internal bracing of the slatted cabin walls creates natural shelving areas where we can stash our collection of books.

All of our furniture has built-in storage as well. Our tables are made from old wooden shipping crates, so the plates and cutlery live inside the dining table. The crate we use as a coffee table holds toilet paper and cleaning supplies.

As a creative type, I think art belongs everywhere. From the throw pillows to the furniture, I love incorporating bright, bold colors. While bold colors might not be your thing, I do encourage you to use every possible outlet for self-expression: your countertops, your rugs, your pillows and bed sheets, your towels, and even the stain or paint you use on your wood surfaces. All of these are opportunities for a little personalization.

Some people feel that hanging artwork in a tiny house is competing with nature, but I find this to be a matter of personal taste. I love nature, and I very much cherish having the ability to take in some breathtaking views. But, at the same time, I have a lot of handmade art that is very meaningful to me. My plants are in pots made by my friend Eve, and some of them hang from macrame gifted to me by my friend Jess. These plants not only provide inspiration and create bright, cheerful spots in my home, but they hold the memories I've created with my loved ones. Plus, they do their part to keep the air fresh and clean in our tiny space.

Yes, it is easy to quickly overwhelm your tiny living area with too much art, but I think that it's very possible to demonstrate your aesthetic in functional pieces.

Another concept that you may wish to embrace is relocating the furniture between day and night. If you've ever been in a large RV, you'll know that many are equipped with seating areas that fold out into beds or benches that push out mechanically to become sleeping areas. You can apply that same convertible vibe to your tiny house with the right furnishings.

In our home, the tiny loveseat is actually a twin-sized foldout bed. We have two easy chairs upstairs that have tiny little nesting ottomans that tuck under the seat, which can be stacked on top of each other and stashed in the corner before we pull out the Murphy bed. We have a large old steamer trunk that is a closet for hanging clothes when placed on the short end but can also hold sheets and blankets when in a regular, flat position.

You can even create a balance between storage and display. Think about things that you use regularly, like dish towels or coffee cups. If you have a fun collection, you may wish to keep these items out in the open and incorporate them into your decor, rather than trying to find a suitable place to stash them when they aren't in use. You've likely seen the open-cabinet design in magazines or on home and decorating television shows. That's another type of storage that also works as a display.

As you examine the potential furnishings for your tiny home, look not only at the fit but the function. The tiny house lifestyle is all about possibilities and potential and finding opportunities to make things work without taking up a lot of space or resources. Innovation is key, and it can actually be fun to discover new ways to pad your nest without taking up space.

I don't want to overstep my boundaries and tell you how to decorate your home, but I will encourage you to personalize your space so that it feels very comfortable and conducive to what you need in a home. Therefore, my "Rules of Decor" are quite simple:

1. Don't be afraid to express yourself.
2. Consider your natural views and lighting.
3. Put the "fun" into "function" with multi-purpose furniture.
4. Examine every angle and how space and stuff can fit multiple scenarios (such as daytime/nighttime furniture arrangement).
5. Strike a balance between storage and display.

As mentioned throughout this book, this is your dream home. While compromise will be required to some extent, don't let yourself get swept into feelings of *well, this is how it has to be*. You do have a choice in this process, in fact, as we've discovered throughout the chapters, you have many choices.

It can be overwhelming. You may come to a point of saying "whatever" and just going with it. I speak from experience here, since Brad and I were very limited in our choices prior to moving into this particular tiny home. There are many, many things I would do differently if I were purposefully building my own dream tiny home. Not only is hand-washing dishes a point of contention for me, but I also wish the porch was on the back of the house, instead of the front, so I could watch sunsets. It's the little things that mean something in the long run.

But there are equally plenty of things that I have learned from living in this home. There are features that I never thought I could deal with that I actually love, such as having a tiny refrigerator that I have to sit on the floor to pack and unpack. I'm very limited in what I can put in there, and so we've been resisting the temptation to buy food we don't need. Our grocery bill has never been smaller. Thanks to the amazing windows in this house, I have gone days without switching on a lightbulb. Even if we didn't have solar panels, our electricity bill would be next to nil.

It's been a process of discovery, which is why I encourage everyone to keep their minds and their thoughts open. Discovering little ways to make a tiny space feel big is part of the fun. Try not to rush through the process, and let yourself uncover new magic in your new home every day.

CHAPTER 5: *MINI*-MIZING YOUR LIFESTYLE

The next part of the tiny house lifestyle I'd like to address is the day-to-day stuff you might not have thought of yet. From figuring out how to fit your life into a tiny house, to keeping it clean and organized, feeding yourself, and even making room and time for your pets or children, there are a lot of things that took me by surprise when I moved into a tiny house.

You would think that I'd be super-prepared, given that I had been living in a van, but honestly, it was a little confusing. Some parts, like walking to another building to shower, were very familiar. Other parts were deceptively convenient, like having a furnace in cooler weather and having an actual bedroom with a full-sized bed instead of a futon mattress in the back of a van. I say "deceptively," because it's all well and good until you run out of solar power, or you need to change the bedsheets and bang your head multiple times on the steeply angled ceiling beams.

In a regular-sized house, apartment, or condominium, you generally have closets or shelves of some sort to help you stash your stuff. Before I married Brad, I actually lived in an apartment that had a closet door that opened to reveal two additional closets. We learn to take abundant storage space for granted. If it's not built in, we simply run to IKEA or The Container Store and casually set up the freestanding storage unit that fits the space and the needs.

In van life, storage is at a premium, but it's very possible to create space for various-sized bins, containers, and in fancier rigs, drawers and cupboards. We managed to make it across the country several times with six drawers, three large flat bins, two bathroom buckets, and a cooler, which served as our clean clothes, dirty clothes, kitchen, pantry, cleaning-supply storage, medicine cabinet, and refrigerator.

But when we moved into the tiny house, the paradigm shifted entirely. We had kitchen drawers and cabinets built in under the sink as well as a small antique sideboard. As mentioned earlier, the kitchen table, coffee table, and other pieces of furniture were designed for storage. A small antique chifforobe was placed upstairs on the tall side of the room, and various shelves and cubbies were available throughout, thanks to the network of exposed studs and supports.

To fast forward to the good part, we're still using the van as a storage vessel. The bins, which fit neatly under our bed in the van, are too big for the tiny house. The bed isn't elevated in the house, due to the low ceiling, so we can't tuck them there. Instead, we've been putting our seasonal clothing in the chifforobe, and the off-season clothing is stored in the van.

Our cleaning products and bathroom essentials can live in the shower house. There are a few shelves in there, but they do get wet when the shower is on, so we needed to find a way to store our linens and towels in the house itself. Brad had the brilliant idea of putting them all in spare pillowcases and stacking them neatly in the corner. I must admit that I've used a pillowcase full of clean towels as a lounging floor pillow from time to time. In a tiny house, nearly everything has multiple purposes!

As you make the transition, you'll probably have several moments where you're absolutely overwhelmed by how little fits in your new space. Before you throw everything out except a single spoon (a threat I've made many times), I'd like to give you some pointers and advice. I know that these tips won't work for everyone, but I hope I can take just an ounce of anxiety or stress out of your tiny home transition.

Section 1: Reducing possessions and clutter

Let's start with *the stuff*. Your plan of action at this point might be, "Chuck it all. Start over." You are certainly empowered to do that, since it's your stuff, your life, and your money, but what if we dialed it back a few notches and made some smart decisions about your belongings?

Earlier, I recommended noting what furniture absolutely won't work, what might be able to work, and what is very much essential to your lifestyle and well-being. You're going to need to do this with your personal stuff too.

By "stuff," I honestly mean everything—from your books to your lamps and your cooking utensils to your computer monitor and towels. You've already accepted that the knickknacks, geegaws, thingamajigs, and thingamabobs alike will need to hit the road, but you probably didn't think about your wardrobe, the contents of your medicine cabinet, and your carefully cultivated collection of board games.

Again, do not panic. If you're like me, perhaps your heart just skipped a beat when you considered how huge this move is really going to be. But take this opportunity to look around at all of the people who have made the same exact transition that you're about to make. It can be done. It will be done, and you're going to be fine.

Also, before I inspire any more stress or panic, I'd like to take the opportunity to share with you that many people who live in tiny houses have a storage unit stashed somewhere. Even those who are constantly on the move in their THOWs will likely have their Great-Aunt Linda's bedroom set, or their far-too-meaningful-to-part-with collection of primitive cat art tucked away somewhere. I actually have an indoor storage locker in Ohio crammed full of original art created by my friends and family (and me, if I'm being honest!). I have absolutely no room for it, but I will not part with it until I shuffle off of this mortal coil. Therefore, I spent $15 a month for a temperature-controlled locker. If you have the budget and the desire, you are very much allowed to keep the larger things that are very meaningful to you, so don't despair that you'll never see your family heirlooms again.

With that in mind, let's take a look at your stuff. I've created this handy room-by-room chart to give you an idea of some of the things I'm talking about when it comes to "stuff." Please note, this chart is not to be considered all inclusive, by any means, and is merely provided to get your mind organized regarding your stuff. Objects are presented in no particular order.

Location	"Stuff"
Bathroom	Towels, linens, dental-care products, skin- care products, nail-care equipment, razors/personal grooming equipment, hair-care products (including appliances like curling irons, blow dryers, etc.), first-aid kit, toilet paper, menstrual products, trash bin, air freshener, cleaning supplies, rags, paper towels, sponges, bathmat, make up, mirrors
Bedroom	Linens, pillows, blankets of various sizes/ thickness, bedside stand, reading lights, television, books, laundry bins, rugs, books, magazines, more skin-care products, night-time pain relievers, nighttime indigestion assistance, heating pad
Kitchen	Bowls, plates, pots, pans, skillets, griddles, baking sheets and tins, casserole dishes, mugs, glasses, plastic cups, measuring cups, measuring spoons, stirring spoons, serving spoons/ladles/tongs, coffee maker, teapot, filters, reusable container collection, strainer, spatula, trays, napkins, clean-up liquid, sponges, rags, drying rack, toaster, toaster oven, waffle maker, popcorn maker, can openers, bottle openers Also, the food itself: cans, boxes, bags, refrigerated items, dry goods, snack foods, produce, frozen foods
Living Areas	Pillows, blankets, television, books, DVD player, DVD collection, games, puzzles, stereo equipment, CD/record collection, photo albums, framed pictures, souvenirs, candles, coasters, floral arrangements

Office	Desk, computer, mouse, keyboard, monitor, filing system, day planner, pens/pencils, art supplies, printer, printer paper, project/crafting table, craft supplies, chair, exercise equipment, video-game consoles, video games and equipment
Wardrobe/Clothes/Closets	Coats, jackets, pants, shirts, dresses, sweaters, ties, casual wear, pajamas, footwear, sweeper, mop, broom, buckets

It is clear from this chart that some simplification is in order for most of us, especially when heading into a tiny house.

Types of Organization Perspectives

I recommend approaching the minimization process with a purpose-driven perspective. That is, think of what purpose each item serves in your life. If it's something you reach for often, then by all means, make sure it's always within your reach. If it's something that means a lot to you, but you rarely touch it or interact with it, maybe it can head to storage. If you genuinely forgot you had it, feel free to give it a new lease on life through donation or a yard sale.

Of course, most people require a more thoughtful and disciplined approach than I typically take to organization. Therefore, I have a few methods you might appreciate as you attempt to de-clutter your lifestyle and rank your belongings by necessity and want. I have included links in the Resources section to help you learn more about organization as well.

1. **The Capsule Format** - You may have heard of "Capsule Wardrobes." I'm a huge fan of the concept because I'm not very good at coming

up with exciting outfits, and van living has taught me to exist with the absolute bare minimum.

The Capsule concept means stripping down your closet to your bare minimums. You'll keep only the things you wear most often and that can be worn in a variety of situations. This can also be applied to your belongings. Do you have a throw blanket that you love to snuggle with absolutely anywhere? Bring it. Can your throw pillows be used as floor seating? Excellent. Can your dining table also be your desk? Can your desk chair also function as a dining chair or a lounge chair? See how many purposes you can create for as many items as possible.

2. **Traditional Minimalism** - There are actually a lot of interpretations of minimalism, but in its purest form, it means getting rid of anything that isn't 100 percent necessary for daily survival: One spoon. One fork. One knife. One plate. It's a very spartan lifestyle that leaves no room for excess or expression.

Many people find this type of lifestyle freeing, for the same reason they find tiny house dwelling relieving. Tiny living means less stuff. Less stuff means less burden. Less burden means less worry, less responsibility, less aptitude for unnecessary curation of collections, and so on.

You actually don't appreciate how much of your brain is wrapped around your stuff until it's not there anymore. Even if you don't think about the fourteen folding chairs in your hallway closet, you know about them. And once they're gone? You'll feel free from those fourteen folding chairs. You'll never have to move them again. You'll never have to set them up and take them down again. You won't have to worry about one of them breaking right before a big family dinner. You don't have to learn how to repair them or figure out how to replace them. They are gone.

However, there are various degrees of minimalism. Some people choose an area of their life to simplify, such as their wardrobe, their bookcases, their kitchen accessories, etc. Many people are currently hooked on Marie Kondo's concept of "sparking joy." If you don't love it, it's time to part ways with it.

3. **Systematic Reduction** - This type of organization is a process rather than a one-and-done method. If you have a lot of time before you need to worry about packing to move into your tiny house, this is a great way to be sure that you've chosen wisely.

In this process, you set up boxes or bins in each room of the house you're planning to reduce (in this case, all of them). Each time you find something that you've completely forgotten about, put it in the box or bin. Continue this process every day over a span of time—you can start now, if you feel like you've got a lot of stuff to spare—and watch what happens. Notice how often you have to dig through your boxes to find something you need.

Systematic reduction uses the "out of sight, out of mind" principle, which is generally how we end up with a lot of stuff in the first place. I will confess that I did this before our van trip, and I discovered that we had nine bottle openers. They just kept accumulating, because we couldn't find the previously purchased opener. It was truly absurd, but this is the type of thing we, as humans, tend to do when we have a lot of space.

4. **"If it fits" Organization** - This is a really specific type of organization that some of my fellow van friends taught me, but it very much makes sense in the tiny house lifestyle. In this concept, you measure all available space, and you only bring what will fit.

This is a very orderly method and requires a lot of analytical thought and logic to really pull it off, but it makes a lot of sense for those building their own tiny home. If you absolutely know that your largest storage space is eleven inches tall, then that cuts back on a lot of the possibilities. You can spend some time trying to figure out how to make it work or move on to finding a smaller option that will work immediately and without much creativity.

5. **The List** - This sounds like something from a sitcom, but it's very effective, especially if you feel you're not making any progress in your minimization efforts.

The premise is very simple. Grab a box. Open a drawer, open a cupboard, closet, etc. Pull out the notebook or journal that you started. Write down every single thing you see in that spot. Now, at this step, you can either walk away and consider the list, or just go for it and pull the things you don't want or need out of the drawer, cupboard, or closet, and throw it in the box. Give the box a number and jot down that same number on the list.

If you end up needing that item, you'll know exactly where it is. In some cases, just knowing that you didn't want it originally will be enough to allow you the peace to give it up. In other cases, you'll realize you were being overzealous, and you really did need that thing. Either way, you can keep track of your process and progress with a list such as this.

Honestly, there's no bad way to get the ball rolling in organizing your home to prepare for the move to tiny. These are just five methods that have gained popularity among those transitioning to living tiny.

Another thing to keep in mind is that you don't have to live in a tiny house to practice any of these organization concepts. If you're reading this chapter, and you're feeling very anxious, you might not be quite ready to go tiny. Sure, tiny house living will force you to live a much more simplistic lifestyle, but if the actual process of reducing your collection is causing you physical or emotional pain, it may not be the right time. As I've said before, it's best to not do this in a rush, because it is a huge change in lifestyle.

You're not going to be able to fill a closet with toilet paper rolls and have room for your favorite floor steamer. And, if you do, you'll have to sacrifice something else. I've said that tiny house living is about imagining possibilities and being creative, but there truly is a lot of sacrifice involved.

On the other hand, this may be exactly the sign you needed to move forward with your plans. If you're the type who can pack for a weekend trip in a single reusable grocery bag, then you're set. For many people, the lessened financial burden and smaller carbon footprint draw them into the tiny house, but the simplicity of the lifestyle keeps them there.

As you work on organizing and minimizing, be honest with yourself. How do you feel? Energized? Excited? Eager? Restless? Regretful? Confused? All of these are valid emotional responses to any big transition in life, but overall, you should feel more positive emotions than negative. Pay attention to any red flags your mind tries to give you at this time.

Additionally, as you're getting rid of things, remember that there are a lot of options and opportunities for your old stuff. Check around your town for charities that accept lightly used items. Are there any book banks or libraries that might take the books you no longer need? Are there any local schools or after-school programs that can use discarded games, art and craft supplies, or DVDs? Sometimes, thinking about the next life that your old stuff will have takes the pain away from seeing it leave.

Local online sales walls are also a good option for getting rid of your possessions. Porch pickups can be a fast way to move your belongings. Always exercise caution when meeting people in person or conducting cash transactions via the internet, but if you're just looking for a good home for your stuff, this can be a great way to liquidate.

Oftentimes, preparing for a tiny house transition has a lot more steps than we imagine. Getting rid of your stuff and preparing for the simple lifestyle that comes with having less room can be emotional and difficult on many levels. Still, many people feel a great mental release once they unburden themselves from their unnecessary stuff. Take some time here to make sure you follow an organization process that makes sense for you in order to free yourself from the added stress of "breaking up" with your belongings.

Section 2: Keeping your tiny house clean

When you live in a tiny space, any size mess can be a big problem. From odors to insects, it's important to take care of your tiny home.

One of my tiny house tutors told me to think of my new home like a car. Say you're running some errands, and you have a drink in the cup holder. You stopped by the mailbox, and your mail is on your front seat. As you run errands, you put some stuff in the trunk. It's safely stashed back there, not rolling around as you drive. You run some more errands, and now you have some packages in your backseat. Then you pick up your spouse from work. You have to move the mail to the backseat, too, where it gets shuffled under the packages. Also, your spouse was awesome enough to get you a coffee when they bought their own, so now you have three drinks for two cup holders. It becomes a juggling act.

But the second act is what's really important. Let's say your spouse is chomping on some popcorn, too, as an after-work snack. You hit a pothole, and popcorn festively flies everywhere.

When you get home, you can either prioritize unloading the car by what you need most urgently, or you can take the time to empty the trunk, get the packages out of the backseat, fish the mail out from under the front seats, clean up the popcorn, remove all of the beverages, and check for any additional spills.

A lot of us do the bare minimum, thinking we'll take care of the rest later. That's generally because we don't immediately have to deal with the consequences of a car full of clutter and mess. But the next morning, that coffee is going to smell mighty funky. You may have a new family of mice feasting on the popcorn. Months go by, and you start to get late payment notices on the mail that snuck under the seats. Various cataclysmic events occur because you didn't take the time to tidy your car.

The metaphor is spot on. The smells, the clutter, the lost items that were hiding in a stack—it can all happen very quickly in a tiny house.

Now, this doesn't mean you can't take a day off from cleaning here and there. It just means if you are not a naturally tidy person, you will need to work on that in order to successfully pull off the tiny house lifestyle.

Whether you live on a fixed foundation or in a THOW, the bug struggle is real. Any morsel on the counter or sticky spot on the floor is a beacon for critters. Ants and mosquitos are particularly cunning and will use any excuse to come live with you for as long as possible.

How do you plan to clean your tiny house? There are a few concepts that you probably haven't considered if you're used to living in a regular-sized house.

First, ventilation. I'm not saying you can't use ammonia or bleach in a tiny house, but I am saying that you will want all of the windows open for several days after, if you do. "Green" cleaners, or those without harsh odors and chemicals are a great option for tiny spaces for this reason.

Next, your power supply. A lot of us rely on electricity and running water to clean our homes. If you do not plan to have utilities in your tiny home, realize that you are going to need to clean everything by hand. In many cases, that's no big deal—a quick push with the broom out the front door, a hand-scrubbing of all surfaces, and done. However, this can be a big deal if you have any mobility issues, awkward spaces where you can't fully stand up or squat down on your knees, or if you have pets (more on that in a moment).

Then there's the storage of your cleaning products. You definitely don't want to put the detergent in with the meat, so to speak. You'll want to make sure you have an area, preferably something with a door or lid to keep it closed off from air, moisture, and insects, where you can stash your cleaning products. That includes everything from your surface cleaner and disinfectant to your broom or electric sweeper.

The good news is that you'll have less space, which means you'll spend less time each day cleaning and use fewer cleaning products. You'll be able to save plenty of money on cleaning supplies. You may find that your time spent cleaning increases, though, with necessity driving a higher frequency.

What about garbage? Sure, lots of things can be composted or gathered and taken to public recycling. And, if you don't have a lot of stuff, then you likely won't have much to throw away. Waste not, want not, right? Still, many of us manage to accumulate at least a little bit of waste that cannot be composted or recycled.

If you have a THOW, or you're trying to live under the radar, curbside trash service isn't going to be a possibility. Some towns and villages have public dump sites, where you can easily toss a bag or two of your waste into a large dumpster or container. If flying under the radar really is your thing, then you might be pretty good at dropping things off at a gas station or fast-food restaurant as you cruise by. On the other hand, if you're living on a fixed foundation, you might be able to sweet talk your neighbors into letting you borrow a little trash bin space here and there.

But expand the concern a bit: How are you going to gather trash within the tiny house—all of your used tissues, empty soup cans, shredded junk mail, sanitary products, etc. Where are you going to put them until you can properly dispose of them outside of your house? Again, there are odors to deal with and the possibility of attracting bugs and animals. Mice absolutely love it when we humans make donations of easily accessible, shreddable paper.

A small trash can with a lid is a great idea, especially if you can station it easily by the door for immediate removal. Remember, if you put anything outside, it will be summarily inspected in detail by any critter that wanders by, from the neighbor's dog to the local group of raccoons. You likely do not want trash strewn across your lawn, especially if you're trying to be discreet or have found a tiny house community that you really enjoy.

Disposing of everything immediately isn't merely a good idea in a tiny home—it's an absolute requirement. Devise a solution before you enter this new phase of your life to ensure that you don't accidentally invite pests or unwanted attention to your tiny house.

Section 3: Tiny home dining solutions

Feeding yourself is also obviously important, no matter where you live. Human bodies require sustenance and creating an adequate nutritional experience when you have very little space to work within requires a smidge of creativity.

I like to think back to our ancestors, living in tiny dwellings or experiencing a nomadic lifestyle, much like the THOW. They spent all day hunting, gathering, farming, bartering, all for the purpose of survival. They followed their food sources, or they stayed put and made their own as farmers. Their dwellings didn't need a lot of space inside, because they didn't spend a lot of time inside. They didn't need a lot of room for food storage; instead, they immediately used every last scrap for practical purposes.

Today, we spend a woeful amount of time indoors and source most of our food from grocery stores and restaurants. But in a tiny house, there's one really big problem about shopping for groceries: Where are you going to put them?

Expansive gardens and tiny houses seem to go hand in hand, but there can be some complications. For example, where are you going to put your garden in your THOW? Sure, you can do some really cool things with containers, the rooftop, and even the bed of your pickup truck. Are you going to be able to grow everything you need in this scenario? Also, how will you store your fresh produce while you're on the road? You might plan to can extras for the cold season, but how are you going to do that in a tiny house, especially if you choose not to have electricity or running water. It's not impossible, but it will require a lot of forethought and research.

Regardless of where or how you structure your garden, it will need tending. Even the most wild garden will require occasional watering, weeding, seeding, and harvesting. In my experience, growing a vegetable and fruit garden is much easier than keeping an indoor houseplant, but the stakes are much higher. While a withered African violet is very sad, a shriveled up green bean vine or bush means no food.

If you are not experienced in gardening, you might want to try it out before you try to make homegrown products your main source of sustenance. Research what types of plants work well in your area, their sunlight and water requirements, and how to keep them healthy and happy. Find out what the yield is per seed or per plant, so you don't grow too much or too little of any particular crop. Don't forget to research common pests in your area also. I lost an entire crop of tomatoes to a very happy colony of moth larvae and donated my entire herb garden to the local deer. I may have lost food and money, but I gained a lot of knowledge with that particular planting season.

The benefits of gardening are plentiful, but then let's take it inside to the moment you need to store your wares. Do you have a refrigerator or a cooler? Are you going to be able to eat an entire piece of produce in one sitting? This may not be important when it comes to berries or beans, but what about larger produce, like melons, cabbages, or cucumbers. If you can't eat the whole thing, are you going to attempt to save the rest for another day or throw it back in the garden to become part of the circle of life?

The storage situation goes for things you don't produce as well. Shelf-stable foods are great as a backup or for use during the cooler months and can ensure that you have a well-rounded diet. But they also take up space. They generally like to be kept in cool, dry places, and pests absolutely love to dine upon them when you're not looking. Things like pasta, rice, and beans don't take up a lot of space, but you'll definitely want to transfer them into critter-proof containers, such as metal cans or thick plastic tubs.

In a regular-sized house, you might have a full set of durable leftover containers. After each meal, you rinse your plate and package the food that's left into a container that's just the right size and shape for your food before tucking it in the refrigerator. If you choose to include a refrigerator or cooler in your tiny home, this is still very possible and still a great idea.

However, how much room do you have for your reusable containers—both in the cupboards and in the cooler/refrigerator? You may want to keep a handful around for a variety of uses; after all, containers are always helpful for everything from leftover cabbage to broken crayons. This does mean, however, that you'll have to prioritize what you keep in your collection. Resealable bags and foil are great alternatives, but they do create extra waste to deal with. There really is no right or wrong answer for these dilemmas, but it's very important to consider them before you end up with a very expensive piece of cheese and nowhere to store it.

And finally, how about the actual prepping and cooking process? Cooking in a tiny house can not only be complicated but also downright dangerous, depending on what equipment and supplies you have.

Our tiny house includes a toaster, a microwave, a wood-burning stove, an outdoor firepit, and a grill. We also brought along our propane camping stove, which was part of our van setup. Our tiny house, on the other hand, is made of two-hundred-year-old reclaimed timber. We try very hard to do as much cooking outside as possible, simply out of respect for the structure and our safety.

You, on the other hand, may be perfectly comfortable with an indoor hibachi grill in your own tiny home. My first recommendation is that you ensure you have the right ventilation for your cooking methods, which may even be required by local building codes (yes, those again). I also recommend fire extinguishers, smoke alarms, and carbon monoxide detectors, as possible. Having worked in the insurance industry for long enough, a tiny house is very likely going to be a total loss in the event of a fire, but you can do your part to save the living beings just by having these three items handy at all times.

All risks aside, the food you buy should mirror the cooking methods you have available to you. If you only have a fire pit, it is highly unlikely that you will buy a vast array of TV dinners. You can find ways to boil water in a microwave, on a grill, or even on a wood burner, but that might not be conducive to making pasta or rice, depending on your set up. Don't buy anything you can't use or donate to a local food bank, or you'll have the potential for more mess, more waste, and more pests.

Food is a necessity, but feeding yourself in a tiny home can be a challenging experience, unless you're prepared for it. Gardens are a fun way to provide for yourself while reducing your carbon footprint, but a little extra elbow grease will be required. Additionally, you want to make sure you have a safe and critter-proof way of storing any shelf-stable foods. You may wish to employ a refrigerator or cooler to keep food fresher longer too.

Your fifty-piece coordinated mix-and-match reusable container set may not be able to make the tiny house transition with you, but that doesn't mean you can't keep anything at all. Explore the possibilities of having a few reusable containers around as well as eco-friendly options for bags and foil that won't drive up your waste.

Lastly, be mindful of the best way to feed your tiny household. You will need to do some experimentation to find out what works and what doesn't work, based on your lifestyle, house style, and environment. You don't necessarily have to minimalize your meals, but you do want to be aware of the confines of your space and supplies.

Section 4: Tips for children and pets

When Brad and I first announced we were moving into a tiny house, the first question we got was usually, "Oh, you're both going to live there? At the same time?" As a result, I went into the experience very wary of how I might share the tiny space with another human being.

I cannot deny—and I don't think anyone who has ever lived in a small space can deny—that it comes with challenges. Having an upstairs and a downstairs helps, but if I need a moment to myself, I can only find it in the shower house or in the closet with the compost toilet. I have confirmed with people who live in double-loft tiny houses, double-bedroom tiny houses, and even condominiums that tread in tiny house territory that breathing room is at a premium when you share a tiny space with other carbon-based life forms.

Therefore, I have collected some thoughts from the tiny house community regarding sharing your space with children and pets. Perhaps this should be its own book, but I feel like I would need several decades of tiny house living and a doctorate in psychology to write that particular tome.

I have it on good authority from several mothers that your tiny house will never be free of minor messes when there are little ones about. You will step on crayons, LEGO bricks, doll arms, and tiny toy cars … sometimes even if you don't own those items. Things will seem to break more easily because there are fewer places to keep them out of the way. Video games and devices with headphones are a very popular entertainment method because they are handheld and can be stored easily without requiring a lot of room.

However, no matter what you do, all the time will be family time. You will share breathing space at all times with your children. Every parent with whom I spoke recommended setting up a nook or area for the kids to have all to themselves, even if it's only during limited times. I've seen this frequently in van living as well. The kids will have their own bunk, which they can decorate to their own tastes and express themselves freely in that space. Regardless of what the space technically is, it's important for everyone in the household to have some "me space" and "me time."

In many instances, it's appropriate and recommended to expand your tiny household to include the outdoors. You can cook out there, you can work out there, and you can absolutely encourage your children to play out there. Many of the parents with whom I spoke indicated that they like to conduct homeschooling sessions outside as often as weather permits to ensure their kids get fresh air, sunshine, and the opportunity to explore the world.

Outdoor enrichment is one obvious solution to prevent children from feeling cooped up inside a tiny home, but what do you do when the weather doesn't cooperate? One mother explained to me that they like to use these days for visits to museums and science centers, whenever possible, but sometimes it's just a matter of sending each kid to their own space, and Mommy and Daddy do their best to get work done with a full house.

For every tip in this book, one father said to add the phrase, "and your kids, if you got 'em," meaning, for every tip included for your safety and sanity, apply that to the children as well. Every piece of furniture you want in the house, remember you need to provide the same for your children, including dining space, sitting/lounging space, and a sleeping area. Your water and power will be used by you ... and your kids, if you got 'em. You'll have your clothing and their clothing, your bathing supplies and theirs, books, computers, food, dining utensils, the greater collection of garbage ... everything will need a space.

Many THOW families have annexed their truck as a storage space, either with a cap on the bed or built-in bins and lockers. Given that modern trucks are chock-full of storage opportunities, this is a pretty resourceful idea. For those who are on a fixed foundation, consider throwing up a shed or outdoor storage closet for some gear. Either option can be a great place to put children's outdoor accessories, out-of-season clothing, or even surplus shelf-stable food to make as much use of the interior space as possible.

As I've never been a parent, I'll refrain from providing any in-depth parenting advice here for fear of treading into the deep unknown. However, I will say that every parent interviewed recommended keeping the kids outside and active as much as possible. Not only is it great for their development, mentally and physically, but it will keep everyone safe and sane when it comes to those indoor times.

With pets, the most common feedback I received was, "Oh the mess. You wouldn't believe the mess."

Consider all of the pet hair/feathers/droppings/trackings in your house. Now, consider all of the pet hair/feathers/droppings/trackings in your house if your entire living area was the size of your bedroom. If you try any of the experiments I recommended earlier, be sure to include your pet (and your kids, if you got 'em). Litter boxes, crates, terrariums, aquariums, cages, habitats … whatever environment your pet requires, make sure you are ok smelling, hearing, and seeing it at all times.

Bird owners have commented on dropped seeds growing into plants through their floorboards. Fish owners have mentioned that changing tanks in a tiny house is complicated, and sometimes, a fish will "go overboard" in a THOW. Small rodents often make a run for it, and while cats and dogs are often very helpful when it comes to pest control, they also shed uncontrollably, which means sweeping every crack and crevice several times a day.

You'll also need to consider disposing of pet waste, such as litterbox contents or habitat contents. You'll have more equipment and food to store as well. If you have a THOW, where will your pet ride during transit? How about veterinary care? Most states require rabies vaccinations for dogs and cats, so you'll need to stay on top of that, as well as scout out a local emergency vet while on the road.

Sharing your tiny house with a pet isn't impossible; it's just going to require a lot more thought and planning than keeping the same pet in a regular-sized dwelling. Just like children, you'll need to consider their overall enrichment as well as quality of life. Since pets cannot tell us what they like in words, we generally have to gauge their behaviors as a sign of their happiness.

Living in a tiny house with other individuals can be trying at times. Brad and I try our hardest to maintain separate levels of the house during the day since we both work from home. Each of us enjoys journeying outside to work in the fresh air, but bright sunlight and outdoor noises can complicate that at times. Creatively hanging a blanket or curtain in an area is one way to give yourself a little privacy from your spouse or children, but remember that your fortress is highly penetrable, and no solution can keep out all of the noise and activity.

Instead, embrace it for what it is, and look for opportunities to make your time together quality time. Use the resources you have at hand, such as the outdoors, to broaden both the tiny house experience and your space. Whether that means holding class outside, creating outdoor activities for the whole family, or getting really inventive with storage space for household goods, what you lack in interior space, you definitely make up for in ingenuity.

This chapter has likely brought some thoughts to the surface that you had never considered before. In my experience—and in that of other tiny house dwellers I've interviewed—these are all things that don't really manifest themselves in your consciousness until you cross the threshold for the first time. "Everything became real the moment I realized I couldn't bring my hair dryer," stated one friend, who moved to a historic working farmstead with a tiny rehabbed cabin. "I knew I wouldn't need my hair dryer on the farm, but it wasn't even an option."

There are a lot of things that are excluded from tiny house living, although your hair dryer may or may not be one of them. As you pack your belongings for donation or sale, as you consider how you're going to feed yourself, and as you wonder if Fluffy will truly be happy in your tiny house, remember: not everyone's experience is exactly the same.

At the same time, we all have what I now call "hair dryer moments." Like my friend, you'll discover something that simply doesn't work the same way in a tiny home. I absolutely miss my dishwasher, and I miss long hot baths with bath bombs. I know these are luxury items, and I'm lucky to have ever experienced them, but the truth is that we grow accustomed to a way of life, and when that lifestyle changes, we need to be prepared to change with it.

CONCLUSION

As I was writing this book, I kept puzzling over how I would conclude it. Unlike some of the other topics I've explored, this isn't a scenario where I can neatly say, "Well, that's how it's done, have fun!"

Tiny house living is an ever-evolving process for every individual. You become accustomed to waking up and sitting up carefully so you don't crack your noggin on the low ceiling. The sound of the solar panels rattling during a windstorm stops being alarming after a while, and you eventually learn to sleep through the sound of rain or hail pounding on a tin roof.

As the days go by, you stop feeling the need to turn on every light in the house. You find that you can just get by with that one light at the top of the stairs, especially if you work on the east side of the house in the morning and the west side of the house in the afternoon. You learn patterns that work, like keeping the furnace set at the bare minimum so it doesn't run out of power in the middle of a frigid night.

You may find you adapt faster than you imagined. You may discover that you have secretly been ready for this experience your entire life. If you've read through these pages and thought, *I already do that*, then you are far more prepared than many people are for the tiny house lifestyle.

You may also develop some strange habits as a result of your experiences. The glove box in my car is filled with napkins. Since I can't store them anywhere in my house, I impulsively pick them up and stuff them into my glove box. We use rags for cleaning, nose blowing, face wiping, and washing in our tiny house, so having something as luxurious as disposable paper ignites a hoarding instinct in me that I never knew existed.

I hope to have imparted the idea that your lifestyle dreams can come true. There are so many options available that, even when you're confronted with roadblocks, a little patience, research, and creativity can make a new path spring forth.

Hopefully, you'll have plenty of time to prepare for your tiny house transition. While patience is a virtue that many of us fail to practice, in this case, time is a very valuable asset. The more you plan ahead for your experience, the less shock and surprise you'll encounter once you start to get settled into your new home.

There will be plenty of decisions, choices, and ideas pushed onto your plate, and it will be overwhelming at times. Remember that notebook or journal I recommended at the beginning? In many cases, this will be your lifeline. You can fill it with every option, choice, or decision that comes your way. If you do have options written down in your journal, I recommend also noting what your final decision was, why you made it, and when you made it. This may sound like overkill, but it's really helpful to know what was on your mind when you're kicking yourself over a particular unforeseen consequence of your decision.

Tiny house living should be pleasant, but no lifestyle is without its challenges. My hope is that this book has prepared you for at least some of the upcoming process. It will no doubt be stressful, but hopefully it will be largely rewarding. After all, this is your dream, and you are permitted to let it come true to the best of your abilities.

I wish you all the best in your new tiny home. If you're on wheels, may your travels be swift and safe. If you're flying under the radar, may your discretion be your guide. And if you're working with a house full of children or pets, I wish you all serenity and a reliable broom.

With a little creativity, flexibility, and forethought, tiny house living can be exactly what you've always wanted it to be!

RESOURCES

I'd like to preface this section by stating that there are many resources out there for folks who are interested in tiny house living and construction. Much like van living, those in the community are frequently willing to share their stories and experiences, as well as tips and tricks for making it work. Much as we get excited to share "life hacks" online, tiny house dwellers really enjoy finding ways to make their lives easier and more productive, even within the self-imposed limits of a tiny home.

Therefore, I want to say that there really are no bad resources when it comes to learning more about tiny house living. Every point of view is going to be slightly different. Some articles will leave you wanting more information, while others may take a few days to peruse and digest the abundance of detailed information provided. After all, if there's one key takeaway in this book, it should be that building and enjoying your tiny home is a deeply personal experience that deserves serious deliberation.

So please consider these resources simply as a way to get started. I'm not personally affiliated with any of these sites, and I'm not specifically endorsing them. I simply felt that the information contained on these sites is fantastic for getting your feet wet and for providing a variety of perspectives on tiny home living.

Read on and be sure to vet the information you glean from these sites with your own needs and experiences. Remember, even if you're isolated in a tiny house, you're never alone, thanks to the vast online community of tiny house dwellers willing to lend some thoughts, advice, and warm words to you!

Knowledge Base | FAQs

The folks at Tiny Home Builders have provided many online resources on their site, which can be used as stand-alone reference guides or an overall encyclopedia of tiny house information.

This link leads to their Knowledge Base, which is essentially an FAQ about everything tiny house related. Again, I don't know these folks, nor is this an endorsement for their site or products, but the ideas and information reflected in this knowledge base provides a very well-rounded guide to some of the most common questions you'll have about tiny house living—and even some questions you haven't thought of yet.

I placed this link first in the Resources because it's vastly comprehensive, which makes it an excellent place to start and return to time and again.

Tiny House Knowledge Base

https://www.tinyhomebuilders.com/tiny-house-knowledge-base

General Assistance

The following links lead to sites that have a lot of general information about tiny house living. I've included a few different points of view so that you can gauge the similarities and differences for yourself. Each site or blog is compiled by actual tiny home dwellers and can provide you with intimate insights that you otherwise won't appreciate until you've spent some time in your own tiny house.

Tiny Home Builders Help Sites

https://www.tinyhomebuilders.com/help/tiny-house-movement
https://www.tinyhomebuilders.com/blog/tiny-house-questions/

The Tiny House Movement Blog
https://www.rockethomes.com/blog/home-buying/tiny-house

Living Big in a Tiny House
Bryce Langston and Rasa Pescud are based in New Zealand and provide an international outlook to various types of tiny house living. They've started a YouTube channel in which they interview other tiny home dwellers and experience many different tiny house lifestyles. This is a fun resource if you really want to get an idea of how amazingly customized the tiny house experience can be.
https://www.livingbiginatinyhouse.com/tiny-house/
https://www.youtube.com/user/livingbigtinyhouse

Tiny House Construction
As you're aware, this is not a book about tiny house construction. However, you're likely looking for a few resources to get you started in the process of understanding and appreciating various tiny house layouts. The following links provide more in-depth information on the topics of types of tiny houses, building code considerations, as well as details about towing and stowing your tiny house on wheels.

Types of Tiny House
https://www.tinyhouse.com/post/7-types-of-tiny-homes
https://www.tinysociety.co/articles/11-beautiful-types-of-tiny-houses/
https://cozeliving.com/beginners-guide-different-types-of-tiny-houses/

Examples of Tiny House Floor Plans
As stated earlier, this is not an endorsement or recommendation, so always be sure to fully research and vet any house plans that you choose to pur-

chase online. Make sure the project is within your scope, affordable, and will meet your local building code requirements.

https://www.houseplans.com/collection/tiny-house-plans

https://tinyhouseplans.com/

Building Codes

Speaking of building codes, here are some links that lead to information on the topic. I cannot vouch for how accurate all of the details are via each link in the future, but at the time of publication, they did correctly lead to accurate details.

2018 International Residential Code (IRC)

https://codes.iccsafe.org/content/IRC2018/appendix-q-tiny-houses

Interpretation of 2018 IRC

https://buildingcodetrainer.com/building-codes-for-a-tiny-house/

State By State Tiny House Laws and Regulations - Scroll down to link to each state individually.

https://www.moneytaskforce.com/real-estate/tiny-house-laws-state-regulations/

Towing and parking your Tiny House On Wheels

https://www.tinyhomebuilders.com/help/tiny-house-towing-guide

https://www.tinyhomebuilders.com/help/tiny-house-parking-guide

Truck Recommendations

https://www.motorbiscuit.com/trucks-tow-small-house/

Dimension Recommendations

https://www.supertinyhomes.com/tiny-houses/weight-size-without-permit.html

Costs and other Financial Considerations

https://www.tinyhomebuilders.com/tiny-houses/build-your-house

https://www.tinyhomebuilders.com/blog/tiny-house-cost/

https://www.mortgages.com/buying-house-and-owning-home/pros-and-cons-owning-tiny-home

Interior Aspects

Just as there are plenty of things to consider when building and towing your tiny home, you'll need to know the latest and greatest updates regarding the interior. The following links provide tips and tricks for creating, installing, and maintaining the various rooms in your tiny house. While not every layout will work for every house or person living in it, these links provide some interesting ideas and insight to help you prepare for the idea of a tiny bathroom, tiny kitchen, and minimized living area.

Bathrooms

https://www.thespruce.com/tiny-showers-4156387

https://www.supertinyhomes.com/tiny-houses/bathroom.html

https://thetinylife.com/designing-your-dream-tiny-house-bathroom-advice-from-a-full-time-tiny-houser/

Kitchen

https://www.tinyhomebuilders.com/blog/tiny-house-kitchen-design/

https://www.homestratosphere.com/tiny-house-kitchen-ideas/

https://tinyhousehugeideas.com/small-kitchen-ideas/

Furniture Ideas

https://www.livingbiginatinyhouse.com/articles/top-transforming-and-multifunctional-furniture-ideas-for-tiny-homes/

https://www.godownsize.com/tiny-house-furniture-small-space/

Power and Utilities

Again, this is not intended to be a building or construction guidebook, but I do feel that knowledge is power. Before you make any hard and final decisions regarding utilities in your tiny house, here are some resources to help you understand the function, cost, and process to make these things work.

Wiring Details

https://bbtinyhouses.com/how-do-i-get-power-water-to-my-tiny-house-all-about-tiny-house-hookups/

https://tinylivinglife.com/2019/05/how-to-power-a-tiny-home/

The Pros and Cons of Solar Power

The blog post from Thetinyhouse.net is particularly interesting, as it provides two points of view regarding the pros and cons of using solar panels for your power source.

https://www.thetinyhouse.net/solar-powered-tiny-house/

https://thetinylife.com/tiny-house-solar/

Water and Sewage

https://www.supertinyhomes.com/tiny-houses/water.html

https://tinyhouseexpedition.com/the-different-tiny-house-plumbing-options-you-should-know/

More Details on Organization Styles and Options

If you're scared, concerned, intimidated, or stressed out about the transition from a regular sized house into a tiny home, you're not alone. These are some resources to provide you with extra information and guidance regarding some of the organization and minimization tips and tricks mentioned in the book.

While this is true of all of the posted links, I'd like to point out that while the link takes you directly to a page that I feel is a decent resource for each topic, feel free to explore each blog, webpage, or resource in detail. These lifestyle sites provide a wealth of information on a variety of topics, not just getting your tiny house organized!

Capsule Wardrobes/Lifestyle

https://www.amazon.com/Capsule-Craze-Rebecca-Elligton/dp/1735025356/ref=tmm_pap_swatch_0?_encoding=UTF8&qid=1620232576&sr=8-8

https://goodonyou.eco/capsule-wardrobes-create-your-own/

Minimalism

https://www.moneyunder30.com/minimalist-living

https://www.becomingminimalist.com/what-is-minimalism/

https://www.theminimalists.com/minimalism/

Other Methods of De-Cluttering and Streamlining

https://www.lifehack.org/articles/productivity/how-organize-your-life-10-habits-really-organized-people.html

https://www.clutterkeeper.com/organize-tiny-house/

https://thetinylife.com/tiny-house-storage/

Experiences | Blogs

There are quite literally hundreds of tiny house bloggers out there, and I can't possibly name them all. Here are a few that provide a wealth of information on everything from how to make your bed in a tiny house to following folks on their journey into tiny house living.

The last link is a blog round up. I will confess that I'm not familiar with every blog on this list as the site is updated frequently.

https://tinyhousegiantjourney.com/
https://tinyhouseblog.com/
https://thetinylife.com/
https://tinyhousecommunity.com/
https://blog.feedspot.com/tiny_house_blogs/

Communities

As is the case with everything in this Resources section, I don't want to appear to be specifically promoting or favoring one group or resource over another. There are so many tiny house communities online for different niches and preferences that I feel like I can't possibly do them all justice. The following links should get you started, however.

Whatever social media outlet you prefer, Facebook, Instagram, Twitter, Reddit, Tumblr, and even LinkedIn have resources and groups for those interested in and participating in the tiny house lifestyle.

https://www.facebook.com/TinyHouseCommunity/
https://www.thetinyhouse.net/find-local-tiny-house-communities/
https://tinyhouseblog.com/tiny-house/tiny-house-friends-world-just-go-meet/
https://unitedtinyhouse.com/

Reviews

Reviews and feedback help improve this book and the author. If you enjoy this book, we would greatly appreciate it if you could take a few moments to share your opinion and post a review on Amazon.

If you enjoyed reading about Kristine and Brad's transition to tiny house living, be sure to check out the rest of her books. From conjuring up the ideal side hustle to living in a van, Kristine Hudson is eager to share her experiences on the road less taken. Join her for more details on topics that impact anyone, regardless of whether they're living their best #vanlife.

Things Every Lifer Needs to Know

mybook.to/vanlife

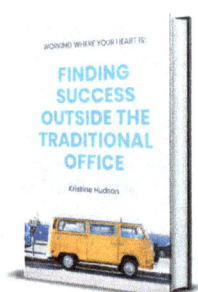

Finding Success Outside The Traditional Office

mybook.to/workfromanywhere

How to Choose the Ultimate Side-hustle

mybook.to/side-hustle

From Wheels to Wellness

mybook.to/Healthinvan

From Wheels to Wellness

mybook.to/youcandoit

www.ingramcontent.com/pod-product-compliance
Lightning Source LLC
Chambersburg PA
CBHW071420070526
44578CB00003B/632